To Jim,

Thanks for all the great times doing program approval reviews and our one tennis outing. I look forward to hitting again.

Hope the episodes in this book remind you of the old days when you were young — er and strengthen

The Village of Poe

your resolve to continue to be a part of the preparation of new teachers.

Clifton

Dec. 9, 2010

The Village of Poe

by

Clifton Dwight Edwards

ISBN 978-0-557-70048-6

The Episodes

Emancipation

And so it came to pass that after 28 years of service during the reign of 4 Governors of the Commonwealth, Monsieur Eduard could labor in the confines of the Tower no more. His joy in serving had slowly been replaced first by disappointment, then by embarrassment and ultimately by shame. The Governor from the City of Brotherly Love had delivered a series of inept opportunistic broom riders to the Tower reportedly as part of an agenda to improve services to the youngest children in the Commonwealth. The first five or six appointees had very brief stays but in December of 2007 the Empress Katrina Shawshank arrived for what turned out to be a two year tenure. In short time, Katrina brought in the Court Bouncer P.T. Barnum and anointed her "Director" and the Chief Court Jester Clara Palina. The three of them, along with a leftover stagehand, Baby Barzilla, orchestrated a modern day version of the Emperor's New Clothes that spread like the old world plague throughout the 94 Towers of Learning in the Great Beyond.

Life for Monsieur Eduard became increasingly difficult. He had not learned to "play the game" and his hopes of outlasting the reign of errors gradually faded. The weekly meetings with Chief Palina more often than not left him in a state of confusion. His best efforts were ignored and his unwillingness to applaud the never ending footage of the Girls Gone Wild left him disillusioned and marginalized.

He attempted to find some meaning in his predicament by taking a week and travelling with his offspring to the mouth of the Mississippi where ineptitude and incompetence had led to widespread calamity several years before. But, his time in the Big Easy only made him realize that the staying power of the political hacks was greater than he had anticipated. As he reflected on his predicament during the 20 hour drive back to the capitol the prognosis for his future looked increasingly bleak.

Upon his return, Chief Palina proclaimed him to be the most unworthy of the Emperor's Court. Her five page mid-year proclamation was by far the worst assessment of his talents that he had ever seen. As he read over the comments of this person whom he had grown to think so little of he began to hear the words "It's time."

During the following three weeks those two words grew from a barely discernable whisper to a never ending scream. There was no escaping it. It was time for his exodus and so he drew up the following Emancipation Proclamation:

Dear Bouncer Barnum,

This letter is to inform you of my resignation from my position in the Department of Education. My official retirement date will be Saturday, April 25, 2009, with my last date of employment being Friday, April 24, 2009.

I began my career in state government during Governor Thornburgh's administration and have survived eight years of Governor Casey, eight years of Governor Ridge, and six plus years of Governor Rendell. I had hoped to end my career at the conclusion of the present administration but the circumstances which I have had to endure since November 21, 2001 when MarzillaJoykilla was assigned the position of Chief of the Division of Teacher Education have slowly worn my spirit down. These circumstances were exacerbated in March of 2008 when Clara Palina was appointed. These two very distinct personalities had at least three things in common: 1) they had no educational or experiential background in the field that they were appointed to the highest civil service position, 2) they had a willingness to do whatever they were told to please the political hacks that appointed them, and 3) they lacked the knowledge and skills needed to command the respect of their staff and the professional education community that we serve. (Working with the two of them could wear anyone's spirit down.)

During the 16 years that I have served in the Bureau, I have had the opportunity to work with some tremendously creative and intellectually vibrant people across the Commonwealth and around the country. I had the opportunity to develop a program approval system that was aligned with the national accreditation process and develop program guidelines that were derived from the Praxis exams and the national professional associations. The process engaged peers in a third party verification review based on the mutual respect of the institution, the review team and the Department. For three terms, 9 years, I was able to serve on national accreditation teams in 15 states from Alaska to Georgia and Vermont to California. I was selected to chair joint national/state teams in Rhode Island, North Carolina, South

Carolina and Georgia. I share all of that to say it has been a blessing and an honor to have had a job that was in so many ways a labor of love and for that I am forever grateful and humbled.

Despite my love for my work, this past year has been particularly difficult because of the political posturing of the Department which I have come to see as nothing short of "bullying" and a contemporary reenactment of the play The Emperor's New Clothes. In the winter of 2005, my former chief appointed a newly hired employee, who had no background in professional education, to take the lead in developing new program approval guidelines for Early Childhood Education, Elementary Education and Special Education. Almost four years and five bureau directors later, those guidelines turned into the "Frameworks" that serve as Act I of the play. In the last six months we have witnessed Act II - the electronic application that pretended to make sense of the Frameworks; Act III – the on-going efforts of the institutions that have been bullied into perverting the academic integrity of their institutions in order to create "programs" that reflect the hundreds of so-called competencies in the frameworks; Act IV – the development of "Tracker Findings" forms for "content reviewers" to pretend that they understand the presentation of the programs; Act V – the "national experts" pretending to "train" the content reviewers to make judgments about applications and finding forms that are only used in PA.

On the afternoon of Tuesday, March 31, 2009, I found myself standing in front of the "4-8 reviewers." The "national expert" who was supposed to be conducting the training was positioned as close to the exit as humanly possible without blocking it. The Chief of the Division was as close to the rear of the group as possible. And there I was, in the final scene of Act V, standing in the front explaining to people about searching and sampling "red, green and yellow" codes and pretending that their confusion would go away once they started writing. That moment combined with the unsatisfactory/needs improvement Employee Performance Rating dated March 16, 2009, which was the lowest of my 28 year career shouted out "It's time."

I thought I could stay for Act VI – compiling the findings from the reviewers and pretending that people so poorly trained could review documents so poorly compiled and make informed judgments and Act VII – contacting the institutions and pretending that after "careful consideration…" but in looking in the mirror and reading the constant barrage of e-mails from the chief, I know "it's time." Giving up my life in 14 day segments in order to reduce my early retirement penalty is offensive to the Giver of my life who has blessed me with great health and a career more bountiful than I would have ever imagined. For that, again, I am eternally grateful. My fear of the coming encore presentations featuring the requirements for the Accelerated Programs, Post-baccalaureate programs, School Nurse, School Counselor, School Principal/Superintendent, ASL, ESL, Adaptations and Accommodations for Secondary and K-12 programs tells me "it's time." Everyone that has been involved has walked away a little less because of their efforts.

In leaving on April 24, 2009 and entering the SERS on Saturday, April 25, 2009 I'm looking forward to working with the institutions in gathering whatever forces can be brought together to bring the play to a halt. Too much energy has been wasted and too many promising careers altered by the willingness of a few political interlopers to alter the landscape of professional education by pretending. It's time!

Gratefully submitted,

Monsieur Eduard

And so it was that Monsieur Eduard left the Tower to seek a new life and new identity. Upon his exit the Court of the Empress quickly locked the gates and banished him from the Tower forever. In the months that followed he heeded the call to journey to the Land Set Aside for Learning, which he had heard about during his years in the Tower. He headed east to find this place and begin life anew as the Groundhog, a creature that would appear from nowhere with no apparent redeeming qualities other than a tenacity for living. This is the tale of his journey.

The Groundhog meets The Prophet

Having been released after 28 years in the Tower the Groundhog set out to begin his new life by travelling to the Land Set Aside for Learning to discover the lessons to be learned from The Prophet and his many associates. The Groundhog undertook his journey with the full knowledge that what he would find in the Land Set Aside for Learning was a world very different than the one he had visited three decades ago and even more different than the one where he lived almost 45 years before. And so, he set out hoping to be able to gain an understanding of the life of The Prophet through observation without evaluation and interpretation. After spending five days in the Land Set Aside for Learning the Groundhog offered the following observations on the life of The Prophet.

The pace of the morning moves very quickly and The Prophet does not. More often than not he watches while his associates engage in conversations, write on papers, rummage through their desks, sharpen pencils, go for water and engage Master Poe with any number of totally unrelated questions and anecdotes. The Prophet remains at his desk most of the time and primarily only engages those that pass by his desk. The engagement is usually very brief and the separation is followed by what appears to be a subdued smile.

The formal part of the morning seems to begin with the "Announcements' from the office but The Prophet and his associates seem to listen to them more as background noise while they do their paper work and listen to Master Poe's daily announcements that occur at the same time. The Prophet watches his associates, who seem to be engaged in almost anything, while he turns pages in books and magazines which he appears to pull out with no particular purpose in mind, based on the amount of time he reviews them. His gaze suggests that neither the office nor Master Poe's announcements require his attention.

The first formal lesson of the morning centered on a story about a Japanese grandfather who took a trip to the United States. The lesson required The Prophet to complete a "K-W-L" chart. The Prophet watched Master Poe introduce the story and give the instructions for completing the chart which was presented on an overhead projector. After the instructions were given Master Poe solicited ideas from the associates about what they knew about Japan. The Prophet offered none and as the associates shared their knowledge and lack thereof The Prophet began to sink down in his seat and lay his head down on his folded arms while continuing to look around. Master Poe brings the discussion to a close and directs the associates to work on the chart independently. At that point The Prophet turns his head down towards the desk so his arms completely surround his face and he is no longer watching.

The Groundhog took this opportunity to wander around the classroom feigning interest in the associates while making his way over to see how The Prophet was faring with the lesson. Upon discovering that The Prophet had not written anything on his paper, the Groundhog suggested that the chart be copied. Much to the surprise of the Groundhog The Prophet, without commenting or making eye contact, immediately drew two almost perfectly straight vertical lines and a crossing horizontal line to make the chart. As instructed, he began to write the question "What do you know?" with "Wha" when Master Poe addressed the associates with directions regarding the pending fire drill. After hearing the directions, The Prophet immediately moved to put the chart away when the Groundhog asked him to at least write "Know" in the first column, which he did. As he continued on to the second column with instructions on writing "What do you want to know?" he wrote "What do" at which point the fire alarm sounded and he stopped writing and moved to get up. The Groundhog suggested that he write "want" at the head of the column. He responded by writing "wan" and quickly shoved the paper into the book and moved to get in line.

The balance of the morning was made up of the fire drill, special assembly, coincidentally about fire awareness, a brief guided reading period, market, recess and lunch. For The Groundhog this morning of the first day in The Land Set Aside for Learning felt like the sounds in an Atlantic City casino and the pace was like a New York City street corner at 8A.M. The Groundhog was in search of a nap and longed for the days of life in the Tower.

The Book Market segment of the morning was divided into three segments that allowed The Groundhog to observe the life of The Prophet. In the first segment of the market the associates were organized into six groups of four self-selected seats. The Prophet sat at the seat closest to the entry way. The Market Woman had placed a different question about President Obama on a small piece of paper on each of the six sets of desks and instructed the associates to go to computers and find the answer. The intent seemed to be for four associates to collaborate in the use of one computer to find the answer but since the number of computers was greater than six those associates that got to the computers first all took one regardless of whether all four came from the same set of tables. In the midst of the confusion, the Market Woman recalled all of the associates back to the tables and assigned each set of tables a specific computer.

The Prophet moved with the associates in his group each time but never in a manner that suggested that he wanted responsibility for operating the computer. At no time did he request to see what the question was that his group was trying to answer. After a little help from the Groundhog the group discovered the answer. One member wrote it on the small piece of paper and the group moved back to the desks. The answer was never shared with the Prophet and he never inquired about it. Once the groups were all back at the desks the Market Woman gave instructions for the next segment without ever asking about the answers to the six questions.

In the second segment of the Book Market period the associates were given oral instructions to find a book to checkout. The Prophet set out walking around the market picking up books and looking at the covers and putting them back. After about five minutes he observed a couple of boys assembled at the door waiting to go to the lavatory. He joined the two and jostled with them while waiting his turn, since only one could go at a time. After about ten minutes the Market Woman requested the associates to reassemble. The Prophet was next to go to the lavatory but returned to his desk with no apparent need to revisit the lavatory question.

Once back at his desk the Prophet became engaged in an argument with the Rabbit while the Market Woman was instructing the class on the written materials that had been placed on their tables. Neither the Prophet nor the Rabbit were paying any attention to the Market Woman and after a couple of exchanges she addressed their argument. The two quickly reduced the discussion to who was making faces or looking at the other. The Groundhog placed himself between the two combatants for about two minutes without addressing either and the exchange stopped. Once the Groundhog walked to the other side of the room the Prophet and the Rabbit engaged in a stare down.

The third segment was brought to a close with no demands made on the Prophet.

Later in the day Master Poe asked the associates to pare up and check each others' three paragraph writing assignment. As the associates regrouped to various areas of the classroom the Prophet walked around the room watching the movement but eventually went to the pencil sharpener without negotiating a paring. He continued to watch the associates while sharpening the pencil and when he was done took a seat in front of Master Poe.

As the associates exited the building for recess they scattered in several directions to play various games. The Prophet entered the yard and stopped as if he had just realized his recess plans had not been confirmed. After looking around for a few seconds he headed over to where the associates were throwing a football with two opposing groups of 8-10 boys. The Prophet placed himself about ten feet from one of the groups and watched the back and forth exchanges without participating. After about 6 exchanges he moved closer in order to participate in catching the ball. Eventually he was able to get the ball which had fallen to the ground. Rather than run with the ball and faking the other boys out until in the clear, the Prophet immediately threw the ball. By doing so he minimized the time that he was in the spotlight at the cost of not making an effective pass.

A similar pattern of behavior was noticed in music class when the Prophet anxiously awaited his turn to play the marimba. Once he took possession of it and the rest of his line focused on him, he was unable to perform the necessary body movements to imitate the rhythm and enthusiasm.

During a math lesson one of the female associates indicated that she did not have any paper. The Prophet watched as the exchange took place and began slowly pulling out his book as if considering making her an offer. By the time the book was completely out of his desk another associate made the offer and he slid the book back in and looked away.

Later in the lesson Master Poe invited the Prophet to hand out the magic markers to the associates. He embraced the opportunity and handed them out appearing to scrutinize which associates got the preferred colors. At the end of the lesson when Master Poe stated that he needed someone to collect the markers, wet boards and some other instructional material the Prophet was too slow in responding and the assignment was given to someone else. The Prophet ignored not being given the assignment and quickly began collecting as many markers as he could before the assignee could collect them, even though he did not have the can that they were to be stored.

When attempting to complete a language arts exercise on similes and inferences the Prophet moved from being attentive and watching Master Poe, to putting his head down and watching the class as they provided examples, to finally keeping his face in his folded arms as the associates were instructed to work independently on the chart. Once his head was down he tossed the handout in front of his desk and onto the floor. When Master Poe did not respond, he threw his textbook onto the floor. At that point the Groundhog made his way around the room to attempt to engage the Prophet.

After positioning himself between Jeremiah and the Prophet, the Groundhog began to discuss the assignment with Jeremiah in a way that ensured the Prophet could hear and hopefully choose to follow along, however, he showed no signs of interest. The textbook was placed on the desk with the comment that it must have fallen on the floor. The Prophet attempted to push the book off the desk again not noticing that the Groundhog had maintained contact with the book. After sensing the resistance he gave up the effort to remove the book but continued to keep his head faced down.

Several days later Master Poe prepared lists of associates that had not completed various assignments and placed them on the chalk board. The Groundhog requested that Master Poe send him the four that had not completed the simile and inference assignment. All of the associates came except the Prophet who stayed at his desks while stating that he had already handed it in. During the ten minute period that the assignment was to be completed the Prophet made eye contact with the Groundhog several times. Each time the Groundhog would motion for him to join them but the Prophet would not respond to the gestures.

Near the end of the period the Groundhog went to the Prophet and asked why he had not joined them. The Prophet, with his legs folded under him in his chair, began to stretch his upper torso across his desk as he quietly asserted that he handed the assignment in. As the conversation proceeded his responses became shorter and ultimately he stopped talking and simply focused on the back of the chair in front of him. At that point the Groundhog left him to his thoughts.

One afternoon the associates were instructed to find a partner to share a writing composition homework assignment. The Prophet stood up and began moving as if he were seeking a partner. The other associates took positions around the classroom some with a single partner and others with two. He circled the room looking but not orally engaging anyone. Eventually he made his way around the room to the pencil sharpener where he stood sharpening his pencil and continuing to watch. Once the sharpening was completed he returned to an area near his desk and seated himself in close proximity to Master Poe. At no time during his brief journey did he appear to take out the assignment that was to be shared.

At the beginning of an indoor recess when the associates assembled into small groups to amuse themselves, the Prophet chose to situate himself with a group of six playing a marble game. He sat on the outside of the group without interacting and repositioned himself several times around the periphery as if to gain a better viewing advantage. The associates did nothing to include him in the order of play and he made no attempt to become a player. After about five minutes he left the group and joined in running around with a group of four associates playing some type of war game.

On three occasions the Groundhog had the opportunity to sit with the associates during lunch. The male associates seem to gather around Moses. Moses has an infectious personality and commands the respect from the others in part by being more assertive physically. The Prophet does not seek to win the favor of sitting next to Moses, instead each day he sits about four associates down but stays attentive to whatever the conversation of the day is about. The Groundhog attempts to pull the Prophet into the discussions by asking him direct questions which he responds to with focused yet minimal information.

In the Village of Poe the window above the radiators are seats of privilege. The associates who claim these seats have to have social skills and a willingness to interact and be seen. The Prophet often watches the associates assemble in the windows where as many as five may climb at one time. Although he has not joined them during the Groundhog's brief observation period, he will momentarily stand near them before retreating to his desk.

From the distance the Prophet's day seems to be a continuous journey through brief periods of attention, less focus and then total disengagement. Sometimes these periods are interrupted by external disturbances of other associates. At other times the Prophet chooses to disrupt the routine of drifting but seldom is the routine broken by activities that celebrate his existence. After observing the Prophet over a two week period his time in the Place Set Aside for Learning appears to be a continuous series of coin tosses whereby the stakes are success or failure and more often than not it comes up failure.

If you can imagine someone viewing the world from the back wall of a one room cabin and watching the events pass by the front window you might get a better understanding of his responses. By the time he sees it, it is passing by and he has to choose to run or let it go. More often than not when he chooses to run and join in it has changed into something else. He then retreats and anxiously awaits the next event with less enthusiasm. He could move to the front window or maybe even stand on the porch but then he would be noticed. The world is always waiting with its spectators who have grown accustomed to the Prophets' efforts or lack thereof. His initial attention suggests that he would like to share the stage and be an active participant.

Life in The Land Set Aside for Learning is new to the Groundhog and the life of the Prophet is one that he has only begun to understand. From these initial observations it appears that in order to help Prophet take control of his life and not retreat to the back wall those around him must make him feel more secure by creating an environment in which he is continuously engaged. At the present time he seems to operate independently from his desk without the walls of continuous engagement. He takes little steps while listening to Master Poe but the floor shifts when the associates speak and his hands come off the railing. When the associates are instructed to go forward he is lost, retreating and it is hard to get him back. As a result of the loss of engagement he rarely will complete a task and seeks solace in the depths of the cabin. In the weeks that followed, the Prophet slowly found his way to the window, the porch and the world.

Like the millions of young associates in the Great Beyond he used his survival skills to surround himself with a cast of characters that valued his anti-social behavior. These characters became known to the Groundhog as "the usual suspects." Their daily antics created an environment in the village that compromised the educational development of all of the associates and made Master Poe's first year a time of continuous questioning.

The Land of Colors

When the Groundhog caught up with the Prophet he and his associates were being escorted by Master Poe to the Land of Colors. Upon their arrival Master Poe instructed them to be silent and lined them up against the wall along the third row of tiles like soldiers marching into Red Square. Today the Most Colorful was absent and Madame Butterfly had come to substitute. Having young associates of her own and having had experience with the Prophet and his associates Madame Butterfly took the "no nonsense" approach when addressing the assembled line. They were to come in without talking, take their seats, a pencil and eraser would be provided, instructions given, questions answered and no one was to touch the papers that had been placed on the tables until they were told. After soliciting the understanding of the associates, she commanded them to proceed into the Land of Colors.

Upon entering the Land the Groundhog immediately noticed the Prophet sitting next to the Rabbit and proceeded to a seat at their table directly across from them, as if they would partake of a meal together. As if on some silent queue the Prophet and the Rabbit began to argue. Madame Butterfly, sensing that this conversation was strictly prohibited, demanded immediate silence with the words "Didn't I say…." The Prophet, not being one with the skills to disengage, jumped up exclaiming, "Tell him to stop talking to me!" Madame Butterfly ordered the Prophet to the ends of the Land to be dealt with in a minute. The Prophet, seemingly surprised by her decisiveness, walked slowly to the outlands with his arms pulled up his sleeves and into his shirt.

After giving instruction to the associates on the project of the day, Madame Butterfly summoned the Prophet to her thrown. She explained her intolerance of disobedience and asked for his willingness to live under her rule. The Prophet began explaining the origins of the confrontation with the Rabbit. This did not please Madame Butterfly so she began preparing a beautiful lime green detention slip, the first the Groundhog had ever seen but apparently not so novel to the Prophet who seated himself on the floor in front of the thrown while the decree was being prepared.

Madame Butterfly came over to share her insights with the Groundhog who was as amazed by her decisiveness as the Prophet. She explained her philosophy of dealing with infidels and her history of previous encounters, ensuring the Groundhog that this approach was most effective in stopping any rebellions. As she talked the Groundhog began moving to the place where the Prophet sat in silence awaiting his sentencing.

When the Groundhog sat down with the Prophet he could see that he was in no mood for discussion. And so, the Groundhog began to share some thoughts about the road ahead, letting go of the last segment, spending your minutes wisely and escaping from the Land of Colors. While seated on the floor the Prophet listened but was unwilling to share. His mind and gaze seemed to be centered on the Rabbit who appeared to be having the time of his life at the table where they once sat together.

For over twenty minutes the Groundhog shared lessons from his own life that the Prophet may have heard in an effort to get him away from the thrown and back into participation in the project. Finally, the Groundhog made him an offer he couldn't refuse, or so he thought. He promised to make the detention go away, to ensure that the Emperor would not be notified of his transgressions and most importantly, that the Prophet's mother would never have to know. However, there was one condition. The Prophet would have to stand up and walk out with the Groundhog.

After much prompting, the Prophet began to show interest in the proposition but somehow the power had been drained from his legs. The Groundhog extended his hand and ensured him that if he took it he would assist him in getting to his feet. Slowly the Prophet allowed the Groundhog to hold his hand but still could not find the strength. Tears began to pour down his cheeks as he inched forward on his knees. As the Groundhog began to stand the Prophet found the strength to go along with him and together they left the Land of Colors.

Once out they immediately came across the Emperor and Master Poe who seemed to have been laying in wait. The Prophet looked forlorn. The escape had been foiled. The promise of the Groundhog was just another ploy. Despite the continued pleading of the Groundhog, without speaking the Prophet changed courses and began walking to the Village to await his punishment. The Groundhog followed hoping to somehow redeem himself for his unintended part in the apparent conspiracy.

After following the Prophet back to his domicile the Groundhog separated himself from the Prophet in order to allow him to reposition himself with his associates without the reminder of how they left Madame Butterfly. The Prophet made his way to his seat appearing to be invisible to his associates. The Groundhog watched from the window and went off to reflect on how the events in the Land of Colors escalated into another loss for the Prophet and yet a small win signaled by the momentary acceptance of his hand.

Later in the day the Groundhog returned to the Village to reconnect with the Prophet and his associates. When Master Poe gives them an assignment to reassemble into small groups to work on a science project, the Prophet and the Rabbit move into separate groups but as fate would have it, in close proximity of each other. Within moments of taking their positions they begin arguing and the argument quickly evolves to the brink of a physical confrontation.

The Groundhog, who was standing less than ten feet from the two combatants, moved between the two and faces the Prophet who is enraged. Master Poe addresses the Rabbit and the associates while the Groundhog talks to the Prophet about the earlier confrontation and the need to let it go. Again, the Prophet chooses to explain the offense by explaining that the Rabbit should not be talking to him and as he speaks his hurt grows with the welling up of his tears and he begins to throw whatever he can get his hands on in the direction of the Rabbit. First it is the pencil, then the small sharpener, then paper, then eraser, then pencil shavings, all the while being careful to throw them in the face of the Groundhog but over his head without hitting him.

When another associate, the Pretender, is inadvertently hit he immediately runs around the Groundhog and Master Poe to exact his pound of flesh by striking the Prophet. The Prophet responds by going after the Pretender but is restrained by the Groundhog until he gives up the struggle. In reality the Prophet is no match for the Pretender. At that point he sinks to the floor in front of the thrown of Master Poe almost in the same position that he assumed with Madame Butterfly in the morning.

Having been summoned at the request of Master Poe the Emperor comes by to see if his presence is needed. The Groundhog assures him that things are under control. For the next hour and fifteen minutes the Groundhog talks with the Prophet about his choices and the power that he must find so that he is not constantly thrown out of the game. The Groundhog searches his body of metaphors and analogies in an effort to bring the Prophet into a better understanding of his own power but the Prophet has retreated to a place that the Groundhog has never been – the Zone of the Unreachable.

As time passes and the sun begins to set, the Prophet begins to move himself, while lying face down, under the thrown of Master Poe. All that remains visible is his upper torso. From that position he began to lift his leg and slowly strikes the under side of Master Poe's thrown. The associates continue with little direct attention paid to the antics of the Prophet. After repeated kicking, the front panel of the thrown fell forward onto his back and head, making a loud metallic sound. The associates are startled but the Prophet makes no move to respond to the panel on his back. Master Poe and the Groundhog watch in fear as the Wanderer goes and lifts the panel off of him. Neither the Prophet nor the Wanderer acknowledges each other.

As the associates began leaving for the day the Prophet began to pull himself from under the thrown and into a kneeling position. Sensing that he was ready to leave, the Groundhog bid goodbye to the Prophet and exited with sadness that this was the Prophet's birthday.

When he retired for the night the Groundhog replayed the conversations, encounters and observations made during his three week journey through the Place Set Aside for Learning and sensed that he had begun to understand the Prophet. It seemed that what the Prophet was looking for is a place called Justice. This is a place where he is affirmed simply because he is and for no other reason. The world he lives in is organized in a way that requires associates to earn this affirmation by being good, or smart, or strong, or funny, or fast, or tall but the gift of the Prophet is hidden. What the world sees is the tenacity with which he demands affirmation from everyone who questions his existence. He defends his right to be from every perceived threat. From the back wall that he watches the world, everyone is a potential threat to his gift.

It is quite probable that at his early age he does not know what his gift is or even that he is in search of it. His eyes tell the Groundhog and anyone who watches that he longs for the place where he is affirmed simply because his existence warrants it. Anyone who questions his right, who asks him to explain where he is going or what he wants, or why he's acting out unconsciously seeks access to the secrets that he hides. In Justice the Rabbit will be treated with the same attention that he receives and not be able to scurry away in the face of authority leaving him to defend his aggravated existence. In Justice he will be able to sit and play and be. The Land Set Aside for Learning is organized as a place where affirmation is earned and the price may be greater than the Prophet can pay. He travels with his baggage and the flip of his coins most often turn up on the failure side. His young battery is already worn down but he continues with his tenacity fending off everyone and refusing to give up. His long journey to Justice is where the Groundhog has to be of assistance.

The Groundhog and Master Poe

After travelling for three weeks through the Village of Poe in The Land Set Aside for Learning, the Groundhog requested an audience with Master Poe to share what he had discovered and reconcile his evolving understanding with that of the Master. During their meeting Master Poe explained how he came to be a Master at the Isle of Messiah which was not far from The Land Set Aside for Learning, and a colony renown for its training. The Groundhog had heard of Messiah and agreed with the Master's assessment.

As the two talked, the Groundhog offered the observation that during his travels he had noticed that none of the other villages in The Land Set Aside for Learning were organized quite like Master Poe's with most of the associates gathered around in a horseshoe with six in the middle. Master Poe explained that when he began his journey at The Land Set Aside for Learning he had setup the posts for the associates in clusters of four but the associates seemed to be continuously distracted and inattentive to his efforts to instruct them. Not long before when the Groundhog first appeared, the village was reorganized in order for Master Poe to provide better oversight and control of the associates.

The Groundhog pointed out that this reorganization demanded an incredible amount of energy because now Master Poe was responsible for controlling the associates who appeared to have little self-control. Throughout the day the level of Master Poe's voice was continually escalating while the associates' ability to drown it out as they went about their way was more and more apparent. Master Poe agreed that his initial requests often went unheeded until they were repeated with increased decibels until they became commands. This was not how he had envisioned his journey to be when he left the Isle of Messiah.

As the two sat and talked they mused about the many associates in the village, as well as the methods used by some of the seasoned masters in The Land Set Aside for Learning. They agreed that there was a large gulf between Master Poe's expectations and what he was willing to tolerate. Associates like the Prophet, the Wanderer and the Rabbit were constantly probing the limits of the gulf as they searched for the intolerable side of Master Poe's limits. More and more associates were finding their way into the gulf and this was wearing away Master Poe's sense of efficacy.

The Groundhog tried to help Master Poe see that his feelings for his associates were a reflection of his self-assessment. His expectations for immediate success as a young master were not being fulfilled. Although he believed in the progressive concepts like cooperative groupings and collaborative learning that were espoused at the Isle of Messiah, he had become intolerant of the associated behaviors and retreated into a Master centered village, but unwilling to institute a total crack-down on the liberties of the associates. However, even though the associates seemed to be running loose more than he would like, they really had not taken over the village.

Master Poe and the Groundhog agreed to take some time to work out a role for the Groundhog to play in creating the village that Master Poe had hoped for. For the Groundhog this would be the place that the Prophet was seeking. The place called Justice where the associates would find affirmation simply because of their membership and Master Poe would share the gifts he developed on the Isle of Messiah.

After leaving Master Poe the Groundhog took some time to reflect on what could be done to help Master Poe close the gulf and transform the village and the lives of the associates who seemed to have lost their way. As he reflected he wrote a list of five ideas to work on:

Reorganize the room so that it is consistent with Master Poe's vision of how he would like it to be and provide the support and a physical presence to those groups that have the most difficulty with the transition. The smaller clusters might make the stage smaller, and therefore decrease the stakes for non-performance, for associates like the Prophet.

Implement a system of consequences for the clusters that encourages the groupings to monitor and control each other rather than Master Poe directing the behavior of every associate.

Establish the rules of the seasons and the time and place for almost everything. Enforce the understanding that the morning announcements and focused reading are a time for listening. Compartmentalize when catch up activities can be done and when assignments are simply too late and not accepted.

Implement a system that demands the immediate attention of the associates without Master Poe raising his voice or repeating his request. Take from the models provided by the best masters.

Encourage the associates to continually reflect on the operation of the village through individual writing assignments and town meetings which allow expression and moderated criticism. Understand that the initial meeting may seem to be unruly.

The Groundhog offered these ideas to Master Poe for further discussion and continued along his journey through The Land Set Aside for Learning. As he walked he smiled and thought about how the challenges of The Land Set Aside for Learning had caused Master Poe to abandon what was in his heart less than five weeks into a journey in which the first leg is 37 weeks and the great masters multiply that 37 times 35 before their work is done. And then he remembered his exit from the Tower which brought him to this place. And again, he smiled.

Sun and Shadows

One morning upon entering the Village the Groundhog was summoned by Master Poe to go to the aid of the Prophet. Since this was the first time the Groundhog was greeted with such a summons he immediately understood the urgency of the request and gave it his undivided attention. From the distance he could see the Prophet reclining forward, knees in his chair and chest on his desk, head looking over the edge of the desk as if contemplating a nap or something crawling in the grass.

As the Groundhog approached, the Prophet feigned not to notice. After exchanging morning greetings with Jeremiah, whose domicile was adjacent to the Prophet, the Groundhog kneeled in front of the Prophet and asked how his morning was going. Receiving no feedback the Groundhog asked who the Prophet had interviewed the night before and how he was progressing on the interview assignment. The Prophet shared the short answers he had written about his interview with his mother. None of the interview answers were written in complete sentences which meant that a lot of work would have to be done in completing the next step of the assignment.

Jeremiah listened as the Prophet spoke and interjected his ideas about similar questions that he had asked his mother. The Prophet seemed irritated by Jeremiah's continuous offerings and would not move on without the prompting of the Groundhog. Although Jeremiah shared more extensive answers about his mother, the Groundhog noticed that none of the shared information had found its way onto his paper. This meant that he too was behind where Master Poe expected the associates to be.

The Prophet and the Groundhog slowly made it through the homework assignment. This surprised the Groundhog because it required a longer amount of attention than he had ever seen the Prophet engage. As they reviewed the final question, "What is special about the person?" the Prophet shared that his mother "played catch and football" with him. He had not written this down the night before but wrote as it came to him. While he was writing, Jeremiah asked the Groundhog if he should get the proper paper in order to write his final copy. The Prophet took issue with the request and shared the four stages of the assignment in great detail: brainstorming, outlining, sloppy copy and final submission. He also pointed out that Jeremiah was only at step two. Jeremiah seemed grateful for the input and turned his attention towards writing. The Groundhog was more than impressed with the Prophet's corrective oratory and understanding of the process and he quietly moved away and enjoyed the warmth of the sun and a small victory.

Later in the day the Groundhog paid another visit to the Prophet to encourage him at the beginning of his work with numbers. On the day before, the Prophet had completed all of the number tasks assigned by Master Poe. The Groundhog was unaware of these skills and asked the Prophet about them. He acknowledged that he liked working with numbers. The Groundhog asked him to do additional work, which he did with the greatest of ease. The Groundhog then asked the Prophet if Master Poe was aware of his skills and the Prophet would give no response despite several promptings. The Groundhog sensed that he had discovered two things that the Prophet wanted to keep secret. So, on this day the Groundhog thought he would carry some of the sun from the day before into another lesson on numbers.

Master Poe began the session by writing a word problem on the board. "Mary wants to buy a rare jewel that costs $150. If she sells one of her stones for $20.56 and another for $60.80, will she have enough to buy the rare jewel?" After praising the Prophet for his previous days work, the Groundhog asked if he could do the problem being written on the board. The Prophet excitedly went about wrote it down. As he writes, Master Poe cautioned the associates that if they were writing it as an addition problem, by adding the three numbers, they were probably going to get the wrong answer.

The Prophet completed the problem and showed it to the Groundhog. The problem was written just as Master Poe suspected. The Groundhog asked the Prophet if he heard Master Poe's warning and he responded, "He said we can't do subtraction!" At that point the Prophet assumed his retreat position lying across his desk. The Groundhog suggested alternative ways of coming up with the answer by adding the lower numbers, as written by the Prophet, and comparing them to the larger number. The Prophet was no longer willing to discuss the subject and slid down in his seat and stretched his legs into the seat next to him. The shadows of other days had returned and he slowly began his journey into the Zone of the Unreachable..

For the next few minutes the Groundhog tried to coax the Prophet into completing the assignment but slowly he disappeared under the desk and stretched out, face down over three chairs. The Groundhog retreated to the back of the village in hopes that the Prophet might pull himself up. After about 5 minutes the Prophet began tossing an eraser into the air. Master Poe had to respond to this because it was a distraction to his teaching the rest of the associates. The Groundhog returned to the Prophets domicile and talked to him about the many metaphors that he had discussed in the Land of Colors. When it appeared that his words were not having an impact the Groundhog told him that he would leave the village for ten minutes and if the Prophet was up when he returned there would be no consequence.

The Groundhog took a walk around the streets of The Land Set Aside for Learning and while walking came across Uhora. She greeted him with news about a plan for the Prophet that had been prepared by Mind Reader. The plan entailed multiple steps for responding to an assortment of behaviors, the most intriguing was "eloping." The Groundhog and Uhora agreed that they would be sure to watch for that one. As they talked the Groundhog asked if the Emperor and Uhora would be comfortable introducing him to the parents of the Prophet. The two of them journeyed to the thrown of the Emperor and requested his advice. He agreed and sent her off to put the word out.

The Groundhog thanked the Emperor and explained the pending situation which he had to get back to in the village. The Emperor decided to come along in case his presence was required. When they reached the village and peered through the gate they could see that the Prophet had not eloped and was demonstrating no behaviors that suggested that he had had anything short of a perfect day. The shadow had lifted and the sun was back in the life of the Prophet.

The Groundhog smiled and slowly moved to his place in the back corner of the village. He recounted the events of the last two days and took solace in knowing that somewhere in the midst of the sun and the shadows, the Groundhog found a way to come away from the back wall of his cabin. He hoped that the two of them had learned a lesson about separating before the door is closed. Maybe there may have also been another lesson about praise and failure and the coin that the Prophet continued to toss. As he mused over these reflections he began to think about the parents of the Prophet and the next few days that he would spend away from The Land Set Aside for Learning with the Council in the Great Beyond.

Big Changes

When the Groundhog returned after three days with the Council in the Great Beyond he noticed that much had changed in the Village of Poe. Upon entering the village the first thing he noticed was that the domiciles of the associates had been rearranged from the large horseshoe configuration to five clusters of four and five associates.

In the front of the village where Master Poe spent most of his time instructing the associates the Wanderer now lived in isolation of the other clusters. His abode was within eight feet of the Master and three feet of the Master's table. In the rear of the village the Rabbit had been relocated, also in isolation of any of the clusters. It was apparent that their locations were designed to minimize the frequent inexplicable journeys of the Wanderer and to expose the Rabbit when he escaped from his lair and ventured into the domiciles of the associates.

Master Poe had given particular attention to create clusters which balanced the brightest and not so bright, the well-behaved and those not so well-behaved and the leaders with the not so readily led. One cluster that truly reflected the insights of Poe included Moses, the Rock, June O'Sullivan and Crown Jewel. The Groundhog looked forward to observing the interactions of such diverse a group of associates.

Even Master Poe's behavior reflected big changes as he gave non-verbal commands to the associates. Master raised his hand, as if to say "Hi!," and slowly some of the associates began to raise their hand in a similar pattern as this gesture spread throughout the village. Several of the associates would request that those talking should stop and pay attention. The Groundhog sensed that the reorganization and non-verbal commands were having the desired affects of developing group responsibility and transferring control of the associates behaviors from the Master to the associates.

Later in the day Master Poe informed the Groundhog that while he was away the Rabbit and the Prophet had come into conflict in the Room of Human Waste. As a result of the conflict both of the associates met with Lt. Uhora and a meeting was planned to bring the parents of the Prophet to The Land Set Aside for Learning. The Groundhog shared that he had met with the father of the Prophet while he was away and that the father had demonstrated some of the "escalating" issues that were observed in the Prophet. Both had the propensity to turn small issues into bigger and more complex discussions that made mutually agreed upon resolution very difficult. Poe also shared that after considerable deliberations efforts were underway to relocate the Rabbit to another village. This saddened the Groundhog who had hoped that somehow the Prophet and Rabbit could be taught to live together.

On the day of the meeting of the parents of the Prophet, many of the guardians gathered. There was the Emperor, Lt. Uhora, Princess Leia, Mind Reader, Master Mind, Easy Reader, Master Poe and two others whom the Groundhog did not recognize. They all gathered around in a large square. The Groundhog sat to the right of the father and the mother sat to his left. The composition of the cast of characters did not bode well as a statement of egalitarian diversity. All of the guardians were from the north and the Groundhog and the parents were from the south. And yet they all came together on behalf of the Prophet.

The gathering lasted several hours. The mother of the Prophet spoke of her love for her son and her frustration at not being able to find anyone to help him. She indicated that she had been in search of assistance since the Prophet first began to visit the Zone of the Unreachable in first grade. The father spoke of his love for his son and his commitment to bringing him into "manhood' while avoiding the mistakes that he himself had made. He spoke of "tough love" and not accepting the "shutdown" episodes but rather demanding that his son stop pretending that something was wrong. He said that his children understood that "all of that stuff had to stop" when he was in the house. The Groundhog also affirmed his love for the Prophet and his belief that somehow the Prophet had come to fear each choice as a win/lose proposition that more often than not turned into a loss. This lost somehow was construed as the loss of love and led to the Prophet retreating into the Zone.

The guardians took turns sharing their concerns and frustrations in helping the Prophet become a productive associate in The Land Set Aside for Learning. Each had their own personal story of efforts to keep the Prophet on the path to greater productivity that somehow fell short. Each stated a resolve to work closer in order to determine why the Prophet continued to choose the Zone of the Unreachable rather participate in the joys of The Land Set Aside for Learning. Easy Reader spoke of six attempts to gage the Prophet's ability at translating the written symbols when most associates could be assessed in one sitting. All of her efforts were thwarted by his retreat into the Zone. After two hours it became apparent that no one knew exactly how to redirect the Prophet and everyone agreed to work more closely to improve communications and develop a rescue plan. They departed leaving it to Mind Reader to come up with a plan.

Jeremiah's Choice

Of all the associates that the Groundhog came to know in his first six weeks in the village, Jeremiah had the reddest hair and the kindest heart. So much so that the Groundhog often pondered whether the blood that warmed his heart and unflappable spirit had to find an additional outlet in his hair and freckles.

One day as the Groundhog made his way through the village he noticed Jeremiah quietly sitting at his domicile, looking as blank as ever and gnawing away at the neckline of his garments. This behavior continued throughout the day as Jeremiah wandered around the streets of the village. By day's end a huge wet v-shaped spot had developed on his shirt from the accumulation of saliva. This eating pattern was new to the Groundhog and so he decided that when the opportunity presented itself he would inquire into Jeremiah's thinking.

As the day came to a close the Groundhog positioned himself along the path that Jeremiah would soon be approaching. From the distance he could see Jeremiah ambling his was to the back of the village. As he passed, the Groundhog asked about how the large wet spot got on his shirt. Jeremiah smiled and shrugged his shoulders while making two shrill short grunts. The Groundhog had come to recognize this motion, which was very common among the associates, as meaning "It doesn't matter," "I don't know" or "I don't care."

The Groundhog pressed the conversation a little further suggesting that surely Jeremiah had some idea of how the shirt became so soiled. Jeremiah smiled again and pulled the crewneck up into his mouth. The Groundhog asked why he would gnaw on his shirt all day. He shrugged and replied "My lips are chapped." The Groundhog could clearly see that Jeremiah's lips were inflamed and as red as his hair. The corners of his mouth now had red lines that made his smile appear to be an inch wider.

The Groundhog suggested that Jeremiah consider using a chap stick. Jeremiah informed him that his mother had given him two. "So maybe you should bring one of them to school" suggested the Groundhog, to which Jeremiah responded, "I have one in my back pack." "And why have you chosen not to use it?" retorted the

Groundhog. Jeremiah shrugged again and gave the two short grunts. "You don't know?" asked the Groundhog. "Surely you have a better answer than that!" Jeremiah looked at the Groundhog and whispered "They might laugh at me."

This thing called "laughter" the Groundhog had come to learn was both a bonding tool, which brought the associates together over the seemingly most insignificant non-sensible ideas like the exchange that he had heard between the boys shouting "I'll slap the taste out of your mouth," and an isolating weapon, the fear of which caused Jeremiah to sacrifice his lips. The Groundhog asked him to consider applying the chap stick in seclusion and cease to suck on his neckline in the days ahead.

The next day when the Groundhog greeted Jeremiah he asked about the chap stick and Jeremiah indicated that he had used it before he left home and placed it in his backpack. The Groundhog suggested that the use of chap stick was not something worthy of laughter or to be embarrassed about. Jeremiah gave his usual shrug and moved along.

Later in the day in the Room for Eating Jeremiah requested the Groundhog sit with him. The day's feast was apparently one of Jeremiah's favorites, chicken tenders. Jeremiah wanted to show the Groundhog how he prepared it. He began by tearing his roll apart and bashing it with his fist on the table until it was flat. Once flattened, he proceeded to squeeze all of the mustard out of a small tube and onto one of the "tenders," and then placed it on the flattened roll. Jeremiah grabbed the flattened roll, a tender and mustard and pushed it into his mouth. Upon closing his mouth the mustard squirted out in one large blob and fell onto his lap. He looked to the Groundhog and laughed while taking hold of another tender and using it to wipe the mustard off his pants and placing it too into his already stuffed mouth. This seemed to make him laugh even more as he displayed all of its contents.

The Groundhog sat in amazement while reflecting on Jeremiah's good nature, the thing called laughter, the eating habits of the associates and the sounds of the Room for Eating where all of the associates came each day and raised their voices to the highest decibels. He was slowly coming to realize how much he had forgotten about the joys of uninhibited eating and the contagious nature of laughing.

Line Leader

At the close of the day, on the Friday following the big meeting with the parents of the Prophet, the associates were assembled by Master Poe on the "second block." This designation was one of the schrules imposed at The Land Set Aside for Learning to train the associates. Many of the guardians required the associates to line up on the second block and walk from village to village as if they were locomotive trains. Great amounts of time could be expended as the guardians watched for anomalies in the lines where associates strayed from the second block of tiles on the ground.

On this particular day, Master Poe designated Jeremiah as the "line leader." Apparently this designation held great prestige because it ensured that the holder of the title would arrive first at whatever destination the associates were sent. However, on this day the Prophet determined that he wanted to be line leader and upon hearing the announcement that Jeremiah would go forth, first among the associates from the Village of Poe, he began his journey to the Zone.

The next ten minutes found the Prophet center stage. First he seized Jeremiah's outdoor garments and back pack and tossed them across the room. When Mo Betta innocently retrieved them, the Prophet rewarded him by striking him in the face and knocking his glasses off. At that point Master Poe reprimanded him and retrieved the correspondence just prepared for the mother of the Prophet in which he was given a "C" for the day. The letter was revised and placed in the Prophet's back pack until he took it out, tore it up, deposited it in the sink and turned the water on. A battle ensued between the Prophet and Master Poe over the rights to the water, which the Prophet had redirected onto the streets of the village. Once Master Poe gained control of the faucet, the Prophet countered by kicking the water already on the floor onto Master Poe. Eventually, the Prophet took flight to his bus with Master Poe in hot pursuit.

Master Poe sent out a signal to the Groundhog to apprise him of the situation. Upon hearing the story, which took place shortly after the Groundhog had exited The Land Set Aside for Learning, the Groundhog was only able to take solace in knowing that at least the Prophet did not retreat into the Zone of the Unreachable. However, the episode led to the Emperor banishing the Prophet from The Land Set Aside for Learning for two days. Prior to his return, Mind Reader would have to develop a behavior plan which included steps for an emergency evacuation once it became evident that the Prophet was entering the Zone.

On the first day of his return Mind Reader met in secret with Master Poe and hatched her plan. The plan called for hourly meetings between the Prophet and Master Poe. During the meetings the Prophet would be required to do a self-assessment of his performance on several variables. Each of them would give a score and the points would be tallied into an overall rating. Mind Reader assured Master Poe of the benefits of such a self-regulating system and as she spoke the Groundhog could hear Master Poe praying that the Prophet would not enter the Zone before he gave his rating. Master Poe agreed to place a hidden camera in the room in order for Mind Reader to see the steps so often taken by the Prophet on his way into the Zone. This plan for the use of the camera only lasted one day without an incident. The behavior monitoring plan lasted much longer but with little success. There were days when the Prophet requested the lowest rating be given even though he had not misbehaved. There were days when he tore up the rating form. And, there were days when he changed the ratings that were given him by the guardians. Mind Reader continued the approach throughout the year regardless of the Prophet's responses.

Peace Be Still

Winnie the Pooh was one of the tiniest associates in the Village of Poe. In fact she was so tiny that she was almost not there. When Winnie stood next to Secret Squirrel and June O'Sullivan the three of them looked like the stick figures often seen on a first graders family portrait. Winnie had a habit of reaching back and pulling her shirt down to cover the four inches between where her legs stopped and her back began. This reinforced the image of the stick figures with a mop for a head.

When Master Poe reorganized the village, the Prophet was moved away from Winnie and Sister Pearlina and Friar Tuck were clustered with her. Undoubtedly, Master Poe was thinking that Winnie's calm presence would balance the unbridled enthusiasm of Tuck. While visiting Friar Tuck the Groundhog came to see that Winnie was one of the brightest of the associates. The quiet way she went about her business set her apart. When given the opportunity to read silently Winnie would bury her head in a book and the world around her seemed to disappear. Even during play in the great outdoors she would engage in the more cerebral activities like table games or writing secrets that only the female associates could view.

One day the Groundhog detected Winnie wearing some newly acquired footwear. He stopped by to speak with her about them and she leaned forward and explained that they were called "Uggs" but hers were "knockoffs" purchased at a footwear store. Having no idea about the complexity of the information, the Groundhog thanked her and she immediately returned to her reading.

On another occasion several of the associates, including Winnie, June, Crown Jewel and Sister Pearlina, had been reported for conduct unbecoming to the associates in the Room of Human Waste. The penalty for the first offense was a "detention point." The accumulation of these points would lead to spending extra time in The Land Set Aside for Learning, which no associate seemed to want.

As the Groundhog passed their cluster Sister Pearlina asked if she could pose a question to him. The Groundhog had come to appreciate Sister as a future attorney-at-law because of the methodical way she would develop her conversations. She had a way of making every moment seem to be bursting with urgency but as the moment unfolded there was this reflective lull that seemed like an eternity. To the Groundhog this was Pearlina's version of "hurry up and wait." And so, he stopped and waited as she formulated the question.

Sister posed a hypothetical about Master Poe's role in defending associates who were wrongfully accused. She shared the pending punishment in great detail and explained that "even Crown Jewel" was under indictment, something that never should happen in a just system. As she made the case for Master Poe's hypothetical intervention to address and clarify the story of the encounter in the Room of Human Waste, Winnie, appearing impatient and irritated by the story, sat up and shouted "It's just a warning on the board so stop talking about it." Pearlina looked over in surprise and Winnie immediately returned to her book leaving no room for further discussion.

The Groundhog moved on with the new understanding that Winnie truly was the quiet voice of reason, not only in the cluster but perhaps among all of the female associates. Although she rarely spoke publicly she was obviously respected. In her own quiet way she ruled and Master Poe's faith in her was already yielding dividends.

Glimmer of Hope

Today the Prophet had an undisclosed episode while being introduced to a new language arts group on consignment with the Soup Lady. The Soup Lady specialized in small group instruction for enhancing the associates' abilities at decoding written symbols. From the Village of Poe she was sent Jada Pinkett, Moses, Friar Tuck and A-Rod. These four associates were as diverse a pack of personalities as humanly possible and the introduction of the Prophet into this group was fraught with danger.

On the one hand A-Rod and Jada came with the charm and respectful personalities that would endear them to any of the guardians. On the other hand there was Moses, constantly pushing to lead and most often going in the wrong direction, and Tuck, a wannabe "gangsta entrepreneur" who could easily talk for an hour about his exploits in beating people up back in Brooklyn. Adding the Prophet to this mix would be a challenging proposition even for a seasoned veteran like the Soup Lady. So, it was no surprise to the Groundhog that on the first day of his entry the proverbial "saliva hit the door."

When the Groundhog arrived at the village Master Poe informed him that the Prophet was entering the Zone of the Unreachable. As the time approached to go to the Book Market Master Poe asked the associates to assemble on block two and the Prophet refused. Master Poe and the associates moved on leaving the Prophet alone with the Groundhog.

Quietly the Groundhog approached the Prophet and asked how long he intended to keep his head buried in his arms. No response was given. The Groundhog shared that sometimes he might reach for a rope and imagine pulling himself out of the hole that he so frequently falls into – but only he could grab it. That suggestion didn't work either.

Soon Lt. Uhora came into the village and informed the Prophet of his "choices," none of which was to remain in the village in the Zone of the Unreachable. She and the Groundhog took turns imploring the Prophet of the urgency of the moment and his responsibility to report to the Market with the other associates or face the consequences of a call to his father.

The Prophet slid from his chair onto the floor and began crawling upright to the door. The Groundhog questioned him about the public display of his crawling through the streets of The Land Set Aside for Learning. When he reached the gate of the village he stood and began to walk in very tiny steps.

Uhora and the Groundhog walked ahead speaking aloud about the need to contact the father, in order for the Prophet to hear even though he was at least 20 feet behind them. Upon reaching the Book Market, Lt. Uhora went on and left the two of them behind. At that point the Prophet went to his knees, blocking the gateway and refusing to enter the Market. The Groundhog informed him that he was going for his phone to make contact with the father. The Prophet responded by lying in the fetal position as the Groundhog went for the phone.

Upon his return the Groundhog found Easy Reader talking with the Prophet in order to get him to move from the entrance. When the Prophet saw the phone he stood and stepped into the Market but did not join the associates. As the Groundhog began to dial, he began to slowly make his way towards the associates and eventually sat with them. Somehow he had made it back from the Zone.

Later in the day, during the study of numbers, the Prophet requested if he could sit in the front directly next to Master Poe and his request was granted. The associates were given instruction on taking a 5 minute test. The Prophet turned and looked at the clock and stated that he could do all of the problems in that time.

Since these tests had signaled the beginning of the Prophets retreat into the Zone the Groundhog moved closer to watch for the signs of the retreat. Much to his surprise the Prophet spent the entire time working on the test and remained more alert and engaged than the Groundhog had ever seen him. At the end of the time with numbers the Prophet handed in the test early and looked to the Groundhog. He asked if he could see some of the books that had been brought in that day. This unsolicited transition from one activity and request was a first and the Groundhog hoped it was a break-through. The Prophet looked through the books and selected one on outer space. He seemed pleased and when he returned to his domicile he shared it with the Drummer and Bobby Kennedy.

The Prophets behavior was a reminder of moments from the days of sun and shadows. As the Groundhog ended his day in The Land Set Aside for Learning he stopped to share the sunny side of the Prophet with Easy Reader. Easy was pleasantly surprised and recounted the experience she had earlier in the day when she found him in the entry of the Book Market. They agreed that despite the early hours somehow the sun had come through.

Further down the road the Groundhog paused to share the sun with Lt. Uhora. Although she was pleased, she also retold her story of dismay over his earlier behavior and the overall state of too many associates in The Land Set Aside for Learning. As they talked, the Groundhog made her see that the sun really did live behind the clouds, even during the current winds of change. They laughed and concluded that indeed this was a good thought to end the day.

Mo Betta

Today Mo Betta wanted to be last. This truly confounded the Groundhog. In the Village of Poe being last was rarely a desirable thing. In fact, throughout The Land Set Aside for Learning and even in the Great Beyond where the Groundhog had spent most of his life, being last was not what anyone hoped for. And yet today, for some undisclosed reason, Mo Betta was determined to be last.

When Master Poe summoned the associates to attention and deployed them to line-up on the second square, the Prophet immediately assumed the position known as "line leader." All of the associates who had already assembled on the second square took a step backwards so that the Prophet's position was not outside of the front gate. Again, this confused the Groundhog because the line leader position was usually reserved for an associate who had demonstrated some type of meritorious character. He had seen very little of this in the Prophet, even on his sunniest days.

Some of the associates like Crown Jewel, Winnie, Two of a Kind and the Pretender seemed to have no interest in the distinction of being the first to arrive at whatever destination Master Poe had assigned to them. Others, like Moses, the Prophet, the Wanderer, Jeremiah and Mo Betta, were in a constant battle to assume the position. Somehow it didn't seem to matter whether where they were going was desirable or not, they would struggle to assemble in a manner that assured that they would get there before the associate behind them. But on this day, Mo Betta wanted to be last.

When the associates were all assembled on square two and began the march to the Room for Eating, the Groundhog noticed A-Rod, Jeremiah and Mo Betta being left behind and seeming to be trying to go in reverse into the wall at the very end of the second square. Mo Betta being the smallest of the three was particularly aggravated by the jostling. In any contest based on sheer physical strength he was sure to lose but his resolve far exceeded the will of the other two contestants. As the associates disappeared out of the gate of the village A-Rod and Jeremiah conceded the victory to Mo Betta and ran to catch the others. Apparently there was no honor in being next to last.

The Groundhog walked along with Mo Betta as they proceeded to the Room for Eating. Mo Betta was wearing the dejected look that he often had when he was walking in the shadows. Since he had just won a hard fought battle the Groundhog thought he should have been looking pleased but he was moping along as if he had the blues. Even more confused about why it would be a good thing to be last in arriving at such a desirable destination and why the blues following the victory, he asked Mo Betta about his day was going in general. Betta replied that he "didn't know."

Needless to say, this response, though very common among the associates, was not very enlightening to the Groundhog. So, he asked him about being last and whether being last made his day better. The response was the same. The Groundhog then asked what would it take to make the seemingly bad day into a good one. Mo Betta's response was, "Change my attitude?"

Mo Betta's words were as puzzling to the Groundhog as his desire to be last. He wondered if he was being taken for the proverbial "ride." How could this insightful response come so easily when throughout his time in The Land Set Aside for Learning he had witnessed Mo Betta have this seemingly continuous intermittent battle with what was known throughout the Great Beyond as the "Blues." The two of them continued along in silence.

The Groundhog began meditating about his time with Mo Betta. As the associates go, Mo Betta seemed more sensitive, easy to please and easy to offend. His best friend, Jimmy Dean, on several occasions had addressed Mo Betta's sensitivity and stopped speaking to him. This only sent Mo Betta deeper into his blues and he'd walk around in quiet befuddlement. He was determined to discover the secret to Mo Betta because when he was not on the verge of the blues the sun would shine in his eyes and reveal a very warm and approachable being. At those times he would often seek out the company of the Groundhog for help with his number calculations and symbolic written language translations. He would share things that he brought from his home in the Great Beyond. The complexity of Mo Betta was truly as perplexing as his desire to be last. The Groundhog began to realize how much more he had to learn about the lives of the associates.

Center Stage

Every now and then in the Village of Poe something happens to shake the very foundation of the village and remind Master Poe and the Groundhog that life in The Land Set Aside for Learning does not revolve around the Prophet. On most days in the village the ebb and flow of life pretty much is consistent with the episode in the life of the Prophet. A good day for the Prophet is a good day for the village. A sunny day in the life of the Prophet is the same for the village. However, there came a day when the alignment of the moon and the sun came under the power of the Wanderer.

If the Groundhog could have read the annals of Mind Reader he would have undoubtedly been able to predict the storm that was coming to the village. On the day before it hit, the Wanderer had engaged Master Poe in a tumultuous battle that ultimately lead to him refusing to assume a position on square number two. After several exchanges with Master Poe the associates pulled out leaving the Wanderer behind in the village with the Groundhog.

After their departure, for some inexplicable reason Moses momentarily returned to assess the situation and confronted the Groundhog about his right to be there. At first the Groundhog was taken aback by Moses' presence but quickly decided to claim his power over the village in the absence of the Master. He declared that Moses return to the associates so that he could give his undivided attention to the Wanderer. Not use to the abruptness of the Groundhog, who after all was just a visitor, Moses puffed up and glared at the Groundhog in defiance. The Groundhog smiled and asked if Moses was thinking about beating him up and if so suggested that the idea should be postponed until he had a chance to eat and give it a little more thought. Moses seemed to hear something of value in the suggestion and proceeded to walk away with fists dangling from his arms, legs spread apart and shoulder rotating as if he were swimming free-style.

The Groundhog turned his attention to the Wanderer and asked why he chose to be so contrary. The Wanderer responded to all of the questions with "I don't know" or questions about Master Poe's motivation for asking anything of him. The Groundhog asked him about the "best advice" that he had been given in life, which the Wanderer had attributed to his father. This advice was about respect for authority, making good choices, and working hard to reach a goal. The Groundhog asked if the Wanderer felt he was honoring the advice. His response was that Master Poe did not show him respect and therefore he did not have to show any to him.

The Groundhog reminded him that a teacher is a gift that should be treasured because his primary purpose was to open his knowledge of the world to the associates. The Wanderer proclaimed that his father had taught him more in one year than he had learned in all of his time in the Land Set Aside for Learning. And then the clouds began to gather when the Groundhog suggested that he talk with his father about his advice and the life he was having with Master Poe. Tears began to well up in the eyes of the Wanderer when he retorted that he could not talk to his father because he did not live with him anymore and did not have a phone number that he could call.

Sensing that this was a common place that the Prophet, Mo Betta, Secret Squirrel, Moses and Friar Tuck often visited in their escapes in the life outside of The Land Set Aside for Learning, the Groundhog took an immediate detour. He asked the Wanderer to consider who was the most valuable gift to the village, he or Master Poe? The response was "I don't know." Then he asked if the associates had to vote on one of them being thrown out of the village who would be removed? To that he said "I don't want to be here anyway." The Groundhog then said that both of you are gifts but your efforts keep the village from enjoying the gift of Master Poe. This time he responded with "So." The Groundhog stated that the village needed Master Poe so much so that if he got sick and could not come the Emperor would have to send a substitute. He asked do you think someone would send a substitute for the Wanderer if he could not come. His response was that he did not care. At that point Master Poe returned to the village to resume his efforts.

And so it came to past that on the next day the Wanderer brought the shadows from the clouds of the pending storm. The day was full of end of marking period tests and during one administration the Wanderer approached Master Poe who was working with two associates. As he approached, Master Poe explained that he would address his concern once he finished with the two associates and asked him to return to his seat. The Wanderer asked "Why?" Master Poe explained that during the test everyone needed to remain seated. Again the Wanderer responded with "Why?"

Master Poe turned from the two associates that he was giving instructions on the test to and asked the Wanderer to "Please return to your seat until I am finished!" The Wanderer turned and took two steps away from Master Poe and towards the chalkboard which was about six feet from his seat. At that point he said "Now can I ask you a question?" From that point on the Wanderer took center stage with a storm of repeated questions and responses from Master Poe. "No, not until you are in your seat." "How come I have to be in my seat?" "Because we are taking a test. So please, I need you to return to your seat." Throughout the performance the Wanderer moved closer to his seat, a distance he could have reached in a single leap. Along the way he occupied another chair, turned the desk around and pulled it to another chair, questioned why the new location was not good enough, sat in his original chair while leaving the desk at the secondary chair, refused to return the desk, and questioned why the desk mattered when the initial request did not say anything about a desk.

During the performance the Groundhog very quietly came to sit near the Wanderer. Upon noticing his presence he asked him "Why are you sitting there?" The Groundhog responded "I don't know." Then a series of repeated questions that went back and forth between "Why are you sitting there?" and "Why are you looking at me?" followed. The Groundhog's response of "I don't know" was coupled with a whisper "You don't have to do this." The Wanderer repeated his two questions several times before he sensed that the Groundhog had the brains of a defiant ten year old and got up and walked over and removed the test from Master Poe's desk. Master Poe responded by calmly taking the test back and the Wanderer stalked out of the village. Master Poe followed urging him to come back but the gate closed and the shadows overcame the village.

During the storm most of the associates continued to work on the test, seemingly undisturbed by the downpour. The Prophet watched with the most attentive eye as if he were studying for a part as a fill-in. Undoubtedly, there were some moves that he was thinking about adding to his already extensive repertoire. Moses took on an active role of storm scout, making his way around the village to visit Master Poe and witness the eye of the storm. Sister Pearlina climb up to seat herself on the back of her chair and as the Groundhog suggested that she remain seated the Prophet immediately moved his rear up the seat as if he thought it was a great idea that he had overlooked. The Groundhog quickly reminded him "not to go there."

While outside the gates, Master Poe summoned the Emperor and Lt. Uhora and the Wanderer was removed stage right. Master Poe returned to the village and some semblance of order was restored. The Groundhog returned to the rear of the village where he discovered June O'Sullivan in tears. Moses exclaimed, with much glee, that the Rock had hurt her feelings. Crown Jewel looked distraught that June was so inconsolable. The Groundhog asked the Rock what he had done. Having been so unaccustomed to being accused of any wrongdoing, the Rock was almost approaching tears for the shame of his transgression, or maybe it was being the dupe to Moses' laughter. He quietly said that he had called her a name as part of a rhyming game.

The Groundhog did not recognize the name which seemed to only have meaning in The Land Set Aside for Learning. He asked was he aware of how offended June was and suggested that he apologize. The Rock quietly said that he was sorry but this did not seem to console June. The Groundhog suggested that he state that he apologize again and this time include what he was sorry about. The Rock seemed a little befuddled but came up with the idea, "I'm sorry that I hurt your feelings." This seemed to work for June who immediately began wiping away her tears. The Groundhog turned to Crown Jewel who had sat in silence throughout the ordeal and said "I know you would never let the names make you cry so you have to help June look beyond them." Jewel just smiled and began packing her backpack. The shadows began to pass over the village.

Father Island

Late one night, at the end of a not so long week in The Land Set Aside for Learning, the Groundhog was seen sitting thoughtfully in his reclining chair. The events of the week were being replayed in his head as he tried to come up with alternative ways that he could have handled the many challenges that were posed by the associates. He searched his memory bank to find some common denominator shared by the associates whose young lives seemed to be spent fleeing from or to the next opportunity to rebel. In this quiet moment of reflection, he prayed that he and Master Poe would somehow find the secret to redirecting the rebellion and divert their energies into more constructive pursuits.

As he stared out the window, watching the world go by, his eyes began to close and his mind slipped away into the world of dreams where he often retreated. Soon his dreams found him moving rapidly through a vertical light funnel, as if he were being beamed aboard a starship. All around him, on the outside of the funnel, there were faint images of men of all descriptions. There were men from the north and men from the south. There were young men, some still almost boys themselves, and there were old men. Judging from their garments, there were surgeons and bus boys, waiters and tellers, gangstas and chefs, musicians and carpenters. There were the homeless and there were those dressed in three piece designer suits. Some spoke Spanish and some spoke Yiddish. All seemed to be moving about in an almost ghostly manner, hurrying to get somewhere but seeming to go nowhere, as if they only resided in the spirit world.

Suddenly, his movement stopped and he found himself walking on the outskirts of a very dimly lit one traffic light town. Off in the distance he could hear a barely audible chant that sounded like the entire town might be repeating a subdued Native American prayer. When he approached the town he stopped to read the large flashing neon-lighted Welcome sign, "Welcome to Father Island the place where boys come to be affirmed by the man of their dreams."

Ever so slowly the Groundhog began to explore the dark streets. As he walked, he noticed the images of the men he had seen while in the funnel. They were now moving about in the air above the small dwellings. Soon he came to a dilapidated looking hovel. He peered through the window and could see the back of a young man walking around in the front room. He immediately recognized the room as one he had played in as a child. On each of the four walls was a large portrait, one of his grandmother, one of his godmother, one of his aunt and one of his mother. Lying flat on the floor were pictures of his father who he hardly knew and his stepfather who had been in his life only from age seven to fourteen. Next to the two pictures was an open photo album which he deduced the young man had been working on. In the quiet of the moment he realized that he was the boy and hurried away.

Soon he came to a small motel with a sign that read "Plenty Good Rooms." The walkway to the lobby reminded him of the entrance into The Land Set Aside for Learning. Once inside he could see that each room had a small window just like the observation windows in the Village of Poe. He proceeded down the main corridor at a very slow pace so that he could look into each room without actually stopping. In the first room that he passed he was startled to see a boy looking back at him but apparently unable to see out the window from inside the room. He immediately recognized the boy as Moses. On a table with a small lamp was a pile of formal documents. The chair was situated in a manner that suggested that Moses had been sitting there, possibly just before he may have heard the approach of the Groundhog. There was only one picture in the room. It was of his adopted family. Moses just stood there with his fists balled up leaning forward looking out the window as if in anticipation of a visitor. The Groundhog moved on.

The next room that he looked in he saw a young man that reminded him of Secret Squirrel. Secret was sitting alone at a small kitchen table that had place settings for four. There were large pictures on three of the four walls, similar to the ones that were in the first hovel. One picture was a family portrait of Secret, his brother, mother and father. The second picture was a single portrait of his mother. The third picture, the one he was staring at, was of his father, stepmother and a baby. Secret was just sitting there staring with tears in his eyes, appearing to be lost in his thoughts.

When the Groundhog peered into the room directly across from where Secret sat he saw the Prophet lying amidst a collection of broken toys and athletic equipment. His eyes had the same look which he had when entering the Zone of the Unreachable. The Groundhog noticed two pictures on his walls. The first was a large family portrait with the Prophet, his father and mother and four siblings. The second was a larger than life image of his father, standing in the middle of a boxing ring, wearing a football helmet while holding a microphone to his mouth and a basketball in the other hand. The Prophet lay on the floor staring at the image.

The Groundhog began to wonder how many of the associates he would see in the motel and hurried along. A little further down the corridor he came upon a room in which he could see Mo Betta lying in a king sized bed staring at the ceiling while holding a pair of scissors. On the floor next to the bed was an 8x10 family portrait that had been cut into small pieces. Above the bed was a large family portrait with Mo Betta being held by his mother and his father holding one of his siblings. Mo Betta's eyes were emptying tears as he studied the ceiling and quietly chanted what sounded like a prayer.

Across from Mo Betta's room he spied Friar Tuck sitting on the small table with his feet in the chair, just as he had seen him so often in the Village of Poe. Tuck seemed to be engaged in as lively a conversation as ever. The Groundhog thought that perhaps someone was in the room with him and that quite possibly he had found who he was looking for on Father Island. He put his ear to the window and listened closely but could hear no voice other than Tuck's. He noticed the large family portrait that he had seen in the other rooms of Tuck, his brother, mother and father. In his hand Tuck held a picture of his father and appeared to be talking to it as if he were rehearsing for a future conversation.

When the Groundhog looked in the last room on the right, he saw the Wanderer seeming to be looking back at him through what he now understood to be a one way window with a mirror on the inside. The Wanderer was whispering a stream of questions while bouncing around and throwing punches like a boxer warming up for a bout. As he pranced and jabbed he whispered "Where have you been? Why didn't you call? Who are you? Why don't you love me? And Why'd you have to go." His questions came as fast and furious as when he did battle with Master Poe and his tears arrived just as quietly. There were only remnants of pictures that were once hanging on the walls in the Wanderer's room.

The Groundhog looked on in silence as the Wanderer stepped and jabbed around the small room. Suddenly a door opened and when he turned he could see the silhouette of someone slightly larger than any of the associates coming towards him from the opposite end of the corridor. By his gait, the Groundhog recognized him to be Master Poe. The two nodded without speaking and went outside into the darkness of the night. Once outside Master Poe disappeared and the Groundhog stood alone watching the images of the men hovering above. He walked on and shortly came to a sign at the edge of town. The sign had fallen to the ground and was partially covered with dust. He cleaned it off and read it under the street light. It said, "Fathers, forgive them for they know not what they have done."

More Ebb than Flow

The Groundhog returned to The Land Set Aside for Learning, excited about the meaning of his dream and determined to discover how he might apply his new found knowledge. While walking up the hill on the main street he spotted a new billboard that had been put up while he was away. The billboard announced the associates that had been recognized as having made the Homework Honor Roll. Seven of the associates from the Village of Poe were listed: Crown Jewel, the Pretender, Winnie, Bobby Kennedy, Secret Squirrel, Two of a Kind and Marie Antoinette. He noticed that Secret Squirrel was the only associate from Father Island on the list. He also noticed that a village that he had not visited had over twenty associates on the list. One day he hoped to visit such a place.

As the Groundhog rounded the corner and headed towards the Village of Poe, he could see the Soup Lady scurrying through the gate with the Prophet, Friar Tuck, A-Rod and Jada Pinkett. For the first time he became aware that Jada was the only female from the village that visited the Soup Lady everyday. He remembered Master Poe sharing that she rarely did any homework and that when asked about it simply shrugged and said "I didn't do it." He noticed Moses being left behind and standing on the corner in his lost warrior pose, as if his opponent had suddenly vanished in the middle of a boxing match.

The Groundhog smiled because the sight of Moses reconnected him with the dream. Moses made eye contact and his lost warrior pose quickly changed into tired warrior as his arms sagged and his chin hit his chest in order to avert his eyes. The Groundhog approached and asked how his day was going. He said "not so good right now." As he put his arm around Moses he said, "Come walk with me and tell me how we can make it better." The two of them continued walking in silence as they entered the village. They passed the Soup Lady as she scurried back to her abode more than happy to have avoided another showdown.

Inside the village Master Poe and the associates were back to their end of marking period tests. The Pretender and Friar Tuck greeted him and he smiled and gave the index finger to the mouth "quiet" sign so that they would not interrupt Master Poe. He assumed his position in the rear of the village and noticed Secret Squirrel with his tiny legs pulled up under him in his chair and his head buried in his folded arms where it often went when he had thoughts related to Father Island. Again the Groundhog remembered the dream and the images of Secret's broken family. He quietly approached and asked how he was doing. Secret, with his I'm going to cry look, sat up and shared that over the weekend his dog "Ace" was "put down" after suffering a stroke earlier last week. He retold the story of how Ace was 91 in dog years, had been hit by a car twice and "nothing was broken," and then had a stroke. After the stroke Ace couldn't do much, "just move his head and eyes like this," imitating a right to left direction.

Secret went on to say that there were places, like Spring Creek, where people go when they have strokes but there were no similar places for dogs. So, his father had him "put down." He shared how if wheelchairs could be made for dogs with motors for them to get around it would not be necessary for them to be put down. He jokingly said that they could have handles that could be controlled by the dog's mouth to enable them to pick things up. The Groundhog asked if he thought Ace would be happy riding around in a wheelchair all day when most of his life he was allowed to run free in the wooded area behind his house. "I guess not" was his response.

As the conversation moved on with Secret sharing a book that he was reading, "Brisinger" by Christopher Paolini, the Groundhog asked how he came to choose such a large book. Secret was sharing his desire to read only "7th and 8th grade books" when Mo Betta came over and interrupted with "Can you help me?" He held a word puzzle in his hands that Master Poe had given the associates. The Groundhog suggested that perhaps Secret could be of assistance, if he had completed the puzzle. Secret immediately responded with "No. I don't get that." The Groundhog asked "Why do you say that?" His response was "That stuff is just work they give us to keep us busy." Mo Betta immediately returned to his abode. The Groundhog whispered that he would be over to help him in a few minutes.

Turning his attention back to Secret Squirrel, he asked how his siblings had taken the loss. Secret shared that he had two older "real brothers" and a younger brother and sister who were his step brothers. He took some delight in sharing what seemed to be a new found awareness that he was no longer the youngest but now the middle child. He explained that the young ones didn't really understand and his older brothers didn't talk about it. At that point something must have told him that he had had enough of the conversation because out of nowhere he asked the Groundhog if he knew of "John Wilcott," the radio announcer. He suggested that the Groundhog should listen to him because he was trying to get people to send messages to "Barack Obama" to "stop him from spending money we don't have and making big bills that we can't afford and not giving Vice President Biden a chance to be President." The Groundhog was surprised by the unanticipated enthusiasm and asked if he liked the President. His response was "not very much." Sensing the revival of Secret Squirrel's spirits the Groundhog departed in order to pay a visit to Mo Betta.

Great Escapes

There are many days in the Village of Poe when the primary pursuit of about a half dozen associates appears to be the Great Escapes. On these days the usual suspects that vie for line leader or caboose, supplement those transition pastimes with activities that almost transform the village into a virtual amusement park in which they travel from one ride to another with total disregard for their purpose in coming to The Land Set Aside for Learning. Sometimes they go one at a time and sometimes they partake in concert. The quests always have a sense of urgency and seldom are carried out without fanfare.

The most popular escape is to the pencil sharpener in the northeast end of the village. The sharpener is fastened to the closet door so that when it is in use makes a vibrating gnawing sounding like an old manual lawnmower. Sometimes the associates can give a long spin that continues until their little hands blister or their biceps cramp. Those who are very skilled at the long rapid turns often watch to see if anyone is looking and beam with pride when they discover that most of the village has been distracted by the noise. Those not so gifted more often then not give it two or three short churns, look around and then repeat the churns. Every once it a while they will pull out the pencil and glare at the point which is seldom sharpened without several performances.

Friar Tuck is especially fond of this escape. He attempts to make this trip several times a day. Usually he'll start out walking east across the front of the Village. When Master Poe spots him and asks why he's away from his domicile he responds "to sharpen my pencil." Poe might say, "And where is your pencil?" To this Tuck could just as easily respond, "Oh yeah, I forgot it!" He'll head back to his domicile and amble his way back across the long trek. For Tuck the journey is just as important as the destination. On those occasions that he manages to arrive with a pencil he demonstrates his skills with the long churn method, flexes his biceps and repeats. Sometimes he can take an eight inch pencil down to six inches before the satisfactory smile comes to his eyes. Since he makes the trip so often, the length of his pencils usually reflect his passion. His Pooh handwriting is undoubtedly related to the same proclivity.

Escaping to the pencil sharpener allows the associates the opportunity to become involved in a myriad of distractions along the way. Tuck heads due east, across the northern frontier, and uses the trip to survey future incursions into the village on his return trip. Moses takes a northeast approach and cuts through the village climbing over domiciles, conferring with associates, and just being a nuisance in general as he exercises his legs. As he walks he usually asks the question several times, "Can I sharpen my pencil?" A negative response from Master Poe inevitably leads to an astonished "I can't sharpen my pencil?" This causes him to pause in the center of the village where he can show his displeasure with the rejection and head back, taking a circuitous route to his domicile. Upon arriving he either gets out another pencil or requests that Crown Jewel sharpen his only one.

A-Rod is also very fond of the sharpener, so much so that many of his pencils are sharpened into little two pointed writing instruments. This allows him to practice his sharpening skills at least twice on each journey. It also ensures that his hand is filthy from the point not in use inadvertently writing on the web of his hand or in the palm. His penmanship is also affected by the diminutive size that he crafts his pencils when he heads north up the eastern border of the village. Unlike Tuck and Moses, A-Rod travels in silence seemingly unaware of the business and affairs of the village. The trip allows him the opportunity to stomp out a few tunes with his feet as if he were trying to break in new shoes or maybe practice some rhythmic tune playing in his head.

On many occasions the sharpener has an apparent overwhelming allure and a pack of associates will gather and battle for access. These periodic skirmishes seem most attractive to the Prophet and the Wanderer and they are quick to join in. Once four or five of them are assembled Master Poe orders all of them to return to their domiciles and the dejected looks and disappointment resembles the last would be riders on a roller coaster at an amusement park that closed while they were waiting in line. As they return to their domiciles their little minds begin to ponder that maybe all the escapes may not closed.

After consulting with other Guardians in The Land Set Aside for Learning about the propensity of the associates to escape to the sharpener in their villages, the Groundhog came up with a plan. Apparently this escape was a problem throughout the land. So, he went off in search of five hand-held pencil sharpeners for the village. Upon his return to the village, he asked Master Poe to declare the sharpener a "forbidden zone" except for ten minutes in the early morning, prior to lunch and at the end of the day. He shared with Master Poe that the next time Tuck was spotted making his escape he would be assigned a sharpener and given responsibility for sharpening all of the pencils of the four associates in his cluster. Other associates that frequented the escape would be envious of Tuck and ask for the same "privilege." The primary offender in each cluster would be assigned a sharpener and the same responsibility. This would remove the rationale for the journey and eliminate the associated disruptions. Master Poe accepted the idea but after a week had not assigned the sharpeners.

The associates' second most popular escape was the journey to the Room of Human Waste. Like most escapes, the young males who vie for line leader and last in line are the primary escape artists. Sister Pearlina and Laura Engels are notable exceptions to this male dominated pursuit. The escapeat times seems contagious. Once permission is granted to one associate the word quickly spreads and others "have to go" or "really have to go."

When Master Poe is involved in the art of teaching he frequently responds to the barrage of requests with "not now" or "not right now." The call and response that follows sounds like a chant, "Not now," "But I have to go," "Not right now," "But I have to go bad," "No, not now!" Suddenly the males begin to prance around, hopping from one foot to the other while grabbing the crouch of their pants. When this persists Master Poe relents and grants permission. The female associates rarely dance in this manner, instead they lean forward and well up with tears in their eyes and head to the entry way. By the time they are there Master Poe motions for them to continue on.

There is a schrule throughout The Land Set Aside for Learning which mandates that only one male associate from a village can go to Room for Human Waste at a time. Some of the Guardians send two in spite of the schrule. The Groundhog came to learn that most schrules are subject to interpretation and more often than not provide easy references for why something has to be denied. Despite the intent of the schrule, at any given time several of the associates from different villages find their way there and find relief just in visiting and walking around. In so many ways it is a rest room for associates that just want to get away from the village for 10 minutes.

After the sharpener and Room, the water fountain provides the third most popular escape. Many of the associates visit the water hole for a cool sip of water or to wash their hands which are always filthy from the little pencils. As they drink or wash they seem to find great amusement in watching the water accumulate in the sink or swirl as it goes down the drain. So fascinating is this occurrence that at times they get mesmerized and forget to turn it off. The Groundhog has noticed on more than one occasion that the Drummer visits the water hole more than anyone else. His visits are longer and always focused on swallowing so continuously that he has to come up gasping for air. His size suggests that there is plenty of water already stored up in his girth and maybe his consumption is not about the escape.

Finally, there is the seclusion of the reading corner located in the southeast end of the village. This popular resort usually is populated by one defector who for whatever reason needs to get away from the other associates. However, once the area is occupied another associate will find it irresistible and head back. Soon you can hear sounds that in no way sound like constructive work and the Groundhog will pay a visit to the locale. The assembly will break up with dissenting comments about who the first settler was. Mo Betta's domicile is not far from this area and the proximity makes him the most frequent flyer.

The need for the associates to be constantly involved in these assorted escape efforts was a mystery to the Groundhog. Choosing to wander rather than be engaged in learning did not seem like a very wise choice for associates who were not fairing well at anything other than being first or last in line. While watching them act out their escapes throughout the day he suddenly became aware that the Prophet only chose the Room, the only escape outside of the village. He wondered about the implication of this phenomenon and looked forward to learning more.

Joy and Pain

Throughout the Great Beyond an annual festival is celebrated to commemorate the bounteous blessings bestowed upon the inhabitants. In the days of the Groundhog's youth the associates in places of learning would engage in performances that reenacted the early conqueror's of the "new world" who had miraculously sailed west to reach east and upon arrival mistakenly claimed all that they had "found" as their own and "shared" it with those that lost it. For their new found bounty they were eternally grateful and established a day of sacrificing turkeys as a way to show their appreciation.

Much had changed during the Groundhogs lifelong journey and 28 years in the Tower. No longer did places of learning openly celebrate this day of expressing gratitude. Even though places like The Land Set Aside for Learning closed the gates on the days of gratitude, it had somehow become "politically incorrect" to call the celebration "Thanksgiving." And so it was that Master Poe organized a feast in which all of the associates would bring something to eat that reflected their eastern and western origins.

In the days leading up to the feast Master Poe began to worry that the anticipated bounty brought in by associates might be less than what their forefathers celebrated centuries before. He asked the associates to make a commitment to discussing the harvest celebration with their parents and identify the contributions. The associates were not very forthcoming. In spite of his fears he held steadfast in his efforts to ensure the success of the festival. Each day more and more of the associates came forth with stated intentions and early on the day of the festival the bounty began to appear as miraculously as the east must have appeared on that early western voyage.

Several parents assembled at the village to divide the labor in providing support for the day's events. There was the father of Two of a Kind, and three mothers belonging to Marie Antoinette, Jeremiah and I'm New. The four of them formed a line behind the table displaying the bounty and waited for the instructions of the Master.

The Groundhog read aloud the story of The Bravest Mouse to the associates, while Master Poe busied himself making an exotic liquid concoction reflective of the Hawaiian Islands and reheating some of the contributions. At the end of the story the Groundhog asked the associates to translate the statement, "Laissez bontemps rollez!" which had been written on the chalk board.

The associates, sensing that the words had something to do with the celebration, began suggesting numerous translations like "We should be thankful for our gifts" and "Have a happy Thanksgiving!" and "It's Thanksgiving time." Their innocently expressed words suggested that no one told them that the festival was not about "Thanksgiving." After about six tries the Groundhog stopped them and gave the translation "Let the good times roll."

Master Poe began the festivities by having the associates stand and share what they had brought and whether it represented their ancestry. Laura Engels shared that she brought "streusel" because she was German. Crown Jewel brought something called "canubiana" because she was Greek. Winnie brought cherry cheesecake pie and mashed potatoes because she was Irish. Jeremiah brought cornbread because his mom made it. Two of a Kind brought a pumpkin roll because that's what she asked her father to make. Marie Antoinette brought sweet potatoes. A-Rod brought patolito. The source of the meatballs was not discernible. The usual subjects that vie for positions in line apparently had little commitment to supporting the harvest.

Finally, Master Poe announced that the mother of the Prophet and the Drummer were bringing additional dishes that were soon to arrive. The Drummer shared that his mom was bringing "apple streusel" simply because it was good. The Prophet declined to share so Master Poe informed the associates that the mother of the Prophet was bringing fried chicken.

The feast began with the girls being served first. Some took all that their plates could hold, while others took very little. Jada Pinkett looked over everything and chose nothing. Her discretion probably contributed to her competing with June O'Sullivan for the smallest of the associates. When the male associates were summoned, they jostled for the line leader position. Somehow being last had lost its allure. The meatballs, patolito and pumpkin bread were in the greatest demand.

As the Groundhog quietly worked his way around the village capturing images of the associates, he noticed the Prophet and the Drummer standing by anxiously awaiting the arrival of their sacrifices. The Prophet stood in the gateway while the Drummer, not being one to miss a meal, stood by his domicile half eating and half waiting.

Throughout the village the sounds of the ravenous gratitude could be heard as the associates cleaned their plates and returned for refills.

After a while the mother of the Drummer arrived with an apple pie-like desert. A space was made at the table for the entrée but the associates were much too involved in stuffing their faces to notice the additional item. Mother Drummer had her son take the desert around to each associate and one at a time they all declined. Disappointment began to spread across the Drummer's brow as he turned the last corner of the village without having encountered any takers. With his enthusiasm slowly vanishing and tears in his eyes he approached the Groundhog, who had not taken time to eat anything. Sensing the urgency of the moment, the Groundhog graciously accepted the offering and helped himself to two extraordinarily large servings. His gesture apparently fell short and the Drummer continued on.

Soon thereafter the Drummer and his mother were seen in the southeast corner of the village. As the Groundhog watched he could see that the Drummer could no longer hold back his tears and began wiping his eyes. The sadness of the moment brought to mind a psalmist from the Great Beyond who once wrote "The things that make you laugh make you cry" and "When you look behind your joy, you'll find your pain." The mother stood by helplessly trying to get her son to not be consumed by the associates' unintended rejection.

Suddenly the Groundhog noticed that the Prophet had disappeared from the post he had been manning in the entryway. He felt certain that he had gone in search of his mother and avoid the possible embarrassment of her not showing up or the fate that had befallen the Drummer. In a short while he returned to the village, walking quickly, with a large aluminum tray, mother trailing 20 feet behind.

When the associates spied the tray a loud cry went up throughout the village, "Chicken!" They all dropped what they were eating, grabbed their plates and headed with great haste to the grub line. It was as if they had been thirsting for this delicacy all their young lives and the coming of the Prophet signaled their deliverance. So great was the allure of the chicken that even Jada Pinkett battled for a position up front and the Drummer abandoned his tears and went for his plate.

Over the next 15 minutes the associates engaged in what appeared to be a chicken eating contest. Each exhibited unbridled enthusiasm with the exception of the Prophet, who positioned himself next to his mother for the duration of the festival without showing any signs of engagement. When all of the chicken was devoured and the associates had their fill of the remaining bounty, the parents departed and Master Poe had them write and share some things that they were thankful. Most shared about family and friends. Moses mentioned that he was thankful for the Groundhog keeping him from having a bad day all day. The Groundhog listened and wondered about the joy and pain displayed by the associates during the celebration and in their young lives. He left the village thankful for the lessons he was learning.

Tuck's Turn

Today Friar Tuck took his turn in the center of the village. By nature the Friar was a very affable associate. He loves to talk and his favorite conversations center around either of two things: his father or his life as a gangsta in the big city that he resided in prior to coming to The Land Set Aside for Learning. Tales of his father most frequently provide details of his struggles with villains back in the old city (where he still lives) that either shoot at him or he shoots. His father's businesses are an on-going theme in which lots of money can be made. He recounts how "Sometimes he gets $50 a week or maybe a day" from everyone that works for him. He also owns apartment buildings that people have to pay him for. Friar's father is a karate teacher who has instructed him in multiple ways to attack. When sharing his Karate moves Tuck lifts his right leg about two inches off the floor and kicks as if he were flicking mud off his shoe and then strikes with his left hand in a manner that brings to mind a little girl learning to throw a ball.

Friar's personal battles with greatness seem to have begun when he "got kicked out of second grade for beating up everybody." Upon hearing the stories the Groundhog prays that such deadly force does not manifest itself in the village. As he tells the story, Tuck points to four places on his body where he got "stitches" from the battles, including on his tongue for licking a cold poll. He takes great pride in recounting the details. The Groundhog asked if he new how many stitches he got on his tongue, or his eye, or his arm or leg. Tuck explained that he was young then and "they just told me I got stitches." Because his tongue has a small cleavage and is abnormally large and always bears an excess amount of fluid, the Groundhog wonders whether the poll story is true or a fantasy derived from a movie. Whatever the case, Tuck proclaims that at age ten that part of his life is behind him. Now he wants to be an "entrepreneur."

Tuck's turn began when the Groundhog went to the front of the village to read to the associates today. Master Poe requested that the five associates that visit the Soup Lady come to the rear of the village to work with him on some ideas that they had missed while away. When he began reading he noticed Tuck on his knees rummaging in his domicile in search of a document requested by Master Poe. The Groundhog continued for a while until Tuck's efforts became a distraction. He looked down at Tuck and asked him to quickly finish what he was doing and join with Master Poe. Tuck explained that he was looking for his paper. This revelation was somewhat obvious since he had emptied the entire contents of his domicile onto the floor approximately eight feet in front of the Groundhog.

The Groundhog resumed reading but was interrupted again when Tuck shared his thoughts on the book while the associates were being asked questions. The Groundhog again turned his attention to Friar who was now in an upright crawling position, feigning to be looking into his domicile with all of the contents now on the ground. He reminded him that Master Poe was waiting and that his efforts had become a distraction. A smile appeared on Tuck's face as if he had discovered a well kept secret, the fact that he was now center stage. He straightened his back and went into his oration. "Oh, so I can't find my paper. Well, I can just leave everything here. But why can't I hear the story? How come I gotta go back there?"

The Groundhog could see that Tuck was pleased with his new found power and brought the conversation to a close by saying, "I'm going to move on but you and I will talk about this later." With that he gave Tuck the look that he hoped said to him "Do not forget this moment!" Tuck stood up and began walking as he usually did by yanking his pants up and rotating his shoulders in a manner that resembled an oarsman when viewed from behind.

Later in the day in the Room for Eating Friar Tuck came to sit next to the Groundhog. When he was seated he began talking about his meal and the Groundhog interrupted his monologue by saying "I think you owe me an apology." Tuck replied, "For what?" "For being rude, for being disrespectful, for wasting everyone's time" said the Groundhog. Tuck's expression took on the smile of embarrassment, quite in contrast to the expressions that Moses and the Prophet take on during their moments of conscience. He stated that he was "just looking for my paper." The Groundhog assured him that if he believed what he was saying than he was not as bright as he had thought. Tuck seemed to get it. He replied, "I'm sorry." "Sorry for what?" the Groundhog asked. "I'm sorry for talking strongly to you." was Tuck's response.

The Groundhog was amused, but then not so. He explained that the offense had nothing to do with anyone talking strongly but rather Tuck not doing what he was supposed to be doing and then deciding to draw the entire village into his waste of time. This, he concluded, was "rude and disrespectful" and those words should be included in the apology. Tuck carved out a simple statement, "I'm sorry for being rude and disrespectful." The Groundhog smiled at him and said, "You know that's just the beginning." Tuck stuffed some food in his mouth.

When the associates returned to the village Master Poe instructed them to answer questions in their reading books. Tuck, sensing that it was a good time to test the repaired relationship, called upon the Groundhog to come over and assist him. He asked that the passage in the reading assignment be read to him because he didn't get it. The Groundhog obliged him, in part to show that he harbored no hard feelings and in part because he was not clear on Tuck's reading skills. After reading a page, he asked if Tuck could answer the question. Tuck provided a very rudimentary answer which suggested he understood.

The Groundhog moved on to work in the front with Mo Betta who had been battling the blues all day. As they talked, Tuck began to make his way up to the seat next to the Groundhog. When the Groundhog stood up Tuck exclaimed, "You don't have to go just because I'm coming over. You see friends don't do friends like that." The Groundhog smiled and replied that he had other business to take care of in the village but Mo Betta would be there to work with him.

Soon the day ended and the Groundhog was thankful for the lessons he had learned in the village. He was glad that though Friar Tuck had taken center stage he somehow may have gained some insight into the mutuality of his relationship. He thought about how the Prophet had tried to escape the village and how he and Master Poe, with the threat of a phone call to the father, managed to keep him inside. He recounted his efforts to bring back Mo Betta from his slow dance with the blues and how June O'Sullivan said that she would not sing with him in the Room for Eating because he was married. Somehow he had all of these blessings and more as his reward for escaping the Tower. Still, Tuck's movement towards the Zone of the Seldom Forgiven lay heavy on his heart.

When Doves Cry

Abby Lincoln and Opey G. only visit the Village of Poe to learn about numbers from the Master. Although the Groundhog had noticed Abby on several occasions during his first two months in The Land Set Aside for Learning he had never stopped to talk with her. Opey G. was even less familiar to the Groundhog because his visits to the village had not begun until very recently. Still, the two of them became fused in the heart of the Groundhog as he came to learn of their plight in the bigtop tent of NCLB.

One day the Groundhog spotted Abby leaning over her desk, pretending to do work but never responding to any questions posed by Master Poe who was teaching the associates about "lapsed time." When he sauntered over he could see that rather than calculating numbers Abby was drawing pictures and designs in her notebook. The Groundhog took a seat and watched. Soon Abby realized that her ploy had been foiled and she sat up and smiled. The Groundhog asked what she was doing and her response was "nothing." This had more than a ring of truth to the Groundhog and in her words he could hear the chorus "This is what it sounds like when doves cry."

Sensing that Abby lacked the skills to solve the lapsed time problems, the Groundhog asked her "What is three take away two?" Abby gave it some thought and answered "Zero?" The Groundhog shook his head. Then Abby said "Oh, one!" The Groundhog then asked "What is three from five?" After a brief reflection Abby suggested "Four?" Again the Groundhog shook his head and asked her to think about the answer. She responded, "Two." The Groundhog's spirit swooned like the flight of caged doves flying swiftly but going nowhere.

Later in the day the Groundhog spoke with Master Poe about his assessment of Abby Lincoln. Surprisingly, Master Poe agreed but felt he had to teach the concept of lapsed time because the associates would be "benchmarked" on the materials in a few weeks. Even more surprising was Master Poe's comment that he did not have time to teach her the basic building blocks because of the demands of the other associates and the pace of the curriculum to be delivered at The Land

Set Aside for Learning. As the words flew from Master Poe's mouth you could almost see the dove's crying.

The following day during the study of numbers was when the Groundhog first realized the connection between Abby Lincoln and Opey G. Each time Master Poe posed a time lapsed problem Opey quickly calculated and called out the answer. Throughout his time in the village he repeated this practice of mentally calculating the answer without writing anything on paper or "showing the work." Apparently, showing the work on an hour and a minute chart was as important as getting the right answer on the big "benchmark" that was coming.

The new group of associates that visited the village for the study of numbers was accompanied by Victoria Secret. Victoria was a numbers helper who was a little more than past prime and whose fuse was a lot less than it once was. So, on this day when Opey was offering answers without "showing the work," Victoria became flustered and shouted "You didn't show the work!" Opey replied, "Who me?" as if there might possibly be someone around him that she was shouting at. Victoria, with a look of utter disdain, promptly replied, "No, my mother!" and in the sudden stillness you could hear what it sounds like when doves cry.

Initially the response of Victoria Secret was so surprising that it made the Groundhog laugh so hard tears came to his eyes. Abby, who was sitting next to him, turned with a look of concern and asked if he was o.k. But, his amusement was so great that he had to leave the village in order to regain his composure.

Later in the day the Groundhog went to talk with the Soup Lady about the concerns of Abby and Opey. The Soup Lady suggested that what was happening was not unique to the Village but in fact was happening throughout The Land Set Aside for Learning and beyond. It was her opinion that the need to push on in Abby's case was forced by the belief that the big test would cover materials that would be missed if Master Poe stopped to help her and this would put the other associates in The Land Set Aside for Learning at a disadvantage. At the same time, the need to force Opey to express how he came to his understanding was more important than the accuracy of his understanding was based on what the big test would require. She agreed that this preoccupation with the big test was adversely affecting both the associates and the guardians.

The Groundhog left the company of the Soup Lady a little better informed but a little more dismayed. Upon entering the village he went to sit with Opey and asked him a series of questions. He asked what time was it, what time will it be in 25 minutes and what time was it a half hour ago. Opey immediately answered the questions correctly. The Groundhog smiled and said, "You're going to be o.k." As he moved to the back of the village he spotted Abby cranking out answers with her fingers. They exchanged smiles.

At the end of the day the Groundhog quietly sat reflecting on the lessons learned from the teaching of numbers. During his reflection he imagined Master Poe, Abby Lincoln and Opey G. together in an outdoor tent like those found in zoo birdcages. The Soup Lady stood in front of the tent holding a sign that read "Welcome to NCLB." Inside he saw the image of Abby in the body of a dove jumping off a man made cliff while being told to flap her arms as she plummeted into a pool of water, made to look like a pond. He saw Opey, also in the image of a dove, trying to fly from a high perch beneath a not so cleverly disguised transparent ceiling. And there was Master Poe standing beneath them appearing to be pulling his ears forward in order to hear their cry. Surprisingly, Victoria Secret was absent from the bigtop. He mused that perhaps she had gone to seek the counsel of her mother and avoid the sounds of the doves' cry.

Warrior's Chant

On any given day throughout the Village of Poe the chant of the young warrior's can be heard in response to the call of Master Poe. The chant of defiance is one of the distinguishing characteristics of the male associates. Many warriors sing out the chant as if they are somehow enticing the females into some form of prepubescent mating dance. There are times when as the chant reaches a crescendo the associate on center stage begins to throw himself from side to side in a sporadic rhythmic dance with his shoulders performing a side to side jerking motion as if he were intending to wring himself free of excess water. His eyes roll up into his head and his lips poke out as if rehearsing to kiss Master Poe.

This ritual can be performed while sitting or standing. The jerking of the shoulders is coordinated with the simultaneous movement of the corresponding leg and stomping of the feet when standing. Moses has the greatest ability to do this while seated and can thrust his legs and shoulders with such force that his seat jettisons backwards away from his table. During his initial thrusts his arms become folded across his chest, as if he was expecting the chair to lift off. The Wanderer's chanting expertise is the most versatile and demonstrated while sitting, standing or travelling throughout the village. Unlike Moses, the Wanderer's chants usually begin with a quiet murmur, almost as if he is talking under his breath. His arms quickly fold, consistent with Moses, but rather than rolling his eyes, he squints as if attempting to focus on a tiny particle on Master Poe's forehead.

Like a well choreographed three act children's play the course of the chant is somewhat predictable, although the length of the drama varies greatly, depending upon the mood and size of the audience. Some of the most frequent opening lines are: Can I? How come I? Why can't I? When can I? How come you? Why don't you? Why'd you say? Why do I? But I. Because. I don't wanna! I don't havta. You can't make me. The associates know these lines all too well and can rearrange them with great improvisational skills. On his best day Master Poe has great difficulty coming up with creative ways to respond. There are also days when the associates form a chorus line and seem to join with each other. Master Poe tries to respond with logic and reason and that failing simply ignoring them with expressed exasperation. The third act usually ends with the eyes rolling, shoulders jerking, squinting or storming out of the village. Apparently executions were banned some time ago in The Land Set Aside for Learning and the only recourse is to go after them.

As the Groundhog came to understand the chanting of the warriors he was struck that this pattern of behavior was not practiced by any of the females. Even more surprising was his realization that the Prophet, who rarely gets excluded from the usual suspects, demonstrated very little aptitude for chanting. With the Prophet there seemed to be a couple of hoots and then off to some other form of rebellion, initially there was the descending to the floor but lately he simply offers snide comments. Friar Tuck, as with most things, performed the chant at times with brilliance but more often than not his chants were marked by mediocrity. The chants of Mo Betta were usually limited to engendering a feeling of resignation with limited animation and facial expressions that suggested he was going to bed rather than war. And then there was A-Rod who still had not learned to perform in the big leagues and looked awkward during those moments when his chanting put him in the spotlight and he would quickly exit with a smile, and return to the dugout without fanfare.

One day as the Groundhog entered The Land Set Aside for Learning he stumbled upon the Emperor and the Wanderer engaged in a battle in which the Wanderer was invoking the powers of the warrior's chant. It was coincidental that on the day before the Emperor had spoken with Master Poe about the need to avoid contests with the associates that lead to the summoning of the warrior's oppositional powers. So, on this day as the Wanderer's tiny shoulders began to sway and the rhythm began to lift his spirits, the Groundhog could see that the Emperor was about to be visited by the spirits of the unknown from the Zone of the Unreachable.

During the next 15 minutes the Emperor attempted to send the Wanderer back to the Village of Poe. The Wanderer was more interested in going nowhere and certainly not at the command of the Emperor who continuously gave him choices and a "count to five" time limit. The ninety feet journey down the streets of The Land Set Aside for Learning seemed to exhaust the Emperor and his counting to five was repeated enough times to confound even the most avid numbers cruncher. Finally the Wanderer's chant turned to tears and whaling and his shrugs of defiance were reduced to kicking the walls of The Land Set Aside for Learning, but his resolve was not diminished. At the same time the Emperor had come to the end of his proverbial rope. The Wanderer was in no condition to enter the Village and the Emperor had an empire to reign over. Hence, the command to return to the Emperor's court and another "I don't wanta!" Sensing his Waterloo the Emperor did what any emperor would do and no emperor wants to do. He lifted the Wanderer into his wings and delivered him to his court and you could hear the crying of the doves, along with the whining of the Wanderer.

When the news of the encounter got back to the village the Groundhog wondered about the psychological state of the Emperor. The Emperor's choices suggested that he had not taken to heart three of the cardinal principles for dancing with the chanters. One, the chanters' primary goal is to show the guardians that they cannot be made to do anything. Two, the guardians are bound to use logic and reasoning while the chanters only need to perform defiantly. Three, to overpower the chanter with physical force only reinforces the sense of powerlessness that they feel and confirms their belief that might makes right. These principles are taught everyday in the Village of Poe and now the Emperor in his quiet moments was likely in need of counseling from Princess Leia in order to help him overcome his moment of weakness.

The Groundhog found the mystery of why so many male associates, who sought affirmation on Father Island, take such comfort in the chants of opposition, defiance and rebellion, very intriguing. In speaking with My Favorite Martian he was made aware of some writings on the subject of anger. The author suggested that anger was a secondary emotion and that the guardians must attempt to discover the underlying causes in order to use anger as a positive force. Because the chants were more often than not attempts to exert power the Groundhog began to think that the sense of powerlessness might be the underlying emotion.

All of the usual suspects that got involved in the warriors' chant and scrums at the end of the line had experienced the powerlessness of resolving their relationships with their fathers. In Master Poe they may have found a male substitute to demonstrate and develop their sense of power. Their propensity to chant "because they can" could be a sign of their desire to appear strong when the greater forces of the village, The

Land Set Aside for Learning and the Great Beyond seem overwhelming without the support of their fathers.

And so, the Groundhog came to believe that his challenge, as well as that of Master Poe and the Emperor, was to provide a safe place for the associates to develop and not have to feel the need to be so strong. In doing so they would eventually come to learn the saddest of lessons, that logic and reasoning would not reconnect them to their fathers and exercising the greatest physical power would not empower them to give their fathers the boot of a lifetime.

Changlings

In the four weeks that followed the day for expressing gratitude the Groundhog began to sense a major shift in the forces impacting the learning environment of the village. Two significant changes slowly appeared almost as quietly as the changing of the seasons. The Groundhog had not realized it at the time of Tuck's center stage performance but his audition was part of the beginning of bigger changes. The Prophet and Friar Tuck began to emerge in an intimate psychological rendition of Joy and Pain that threatened to take Tuck over to his own version of the Zone of the Unreachable.

On one not so unusual calamitous day in the Village of Poe the Wanderer in a moment of recurring insanity escaped from the village and made his way to the nearest exit of The Land Set Aside for Learning where Master Poe caught up with him and subverted his attempt to lose himself in the Great Beyond. While Master Poe was engaging the Wanderer in considering the futility of his efforts, the Groundhog sat outside the village with I'm New reviewing a lesson on the nature of numbers. From where he sat the Groundhog could see the Master and the Wanderer doing the warrior's dance and at the same time hear the sounds of the village as the usual suspects plotted new adventures.

Sensing the imminent collapse of civil order in the village the Groundhog ended the lesson with I'm New and entered the gates. Once inside he was immediately confronted by Moses who apparently had waited a little too long to execute his escape. The Groundhog inquired about Moses' destination and Moses began the Warrior's Chant with "Why can't I go…." After being denied permission to leave, Moses came up with the not so bright idea of moving the proverbial mountain represented by the presence of the Groundhog. He turned sideways in an effort to squeeze between the entryway and the Groundhog only to discover the weight of the Groundhog was more than his shoulders could bear. He pushed forward against the Groundhog and found the Groundhog's arm transformed into a forklift moving him in the wrong direction.

Not to be defeated by sheer strength, in a moment of seldom visited sanity, Moses took the high road of logic and reason and explained his rights to the Groundhog. He asserted that he had the right to go where he pleased and that the Groundhog did not have the right to touch him. After clarifying his rights, his moment of sanity passed and he returned to the comforts of pushing and squeezing to no avail. The Groundhog informed him that each time his chest came near his hand he was causing the "touching" to occur. Moses was not convinced and continued to move from side to side in the grip of the Groundhog.

In the midst of Moses' prancing and chanting there was a sudden shift of the forces in the universe, as if his chants were finally heard. Out of the depths of his lethargy the Prophet sprung up in his seat and shouted "Let's clap for Moses!" The excitement in the Prophet's eyes had never been so bright. It was as if the moment he had been waiting for had finally come, the day of reckoning, the day that all the associates would rise up and take over the asylum.

The Groundhog, while stifling Moses with one hand, looked towards the Prophet and quietly explained that "This is you! Rather than lying on the floor, this is you standing up. Do you remember anyone clapping for you?" The Prophet did not respond but just kneeled in his seat with a look of total satisfaction on his face as Moses continued to whine "Take your hand off of me. Don't touch me." Suddenly Master Poe entered the village and order was restored as everyone pondered the fate of the Wanderer, who was never to be seen again, at least not for the rest of the day.

In the days that followed the Prophet became more and more energized. He no longer came into the village looking lost and lethargic and half-lying on his desk. At times he actually moved around the room to work in small groups and his silent defiance became vocalized into some of the more common warrior chants. In many ways his metamorphosis was analogous to someone pledging a fraternity and performing the most outrageous acts and then once gaining admittance going out as a recruiter. The Prophet had indeed made a transition and now his primary focus was to recruit Friar Tuck for enrollment in the Zone of the Unreachable.

Master Poe had reorganized the village from the small clusters in which associates were seated facing each other into linear clusters of three and four with everyone facing the front where he most often stood. Seated in the first row of clusters on the east were the Prophet, the Rock and A-Rod. (Talk about a rose between two thorns!) Directly behind them were Friar Tuck, June O'Sullivan and Mo Betta.

Unfortunately, this seating arrangement was perfect for the Prophet's recruitment drive since in his new mode of operation he was always in constant motion even when at his domicile. All the Prophet had to do was turn and look to the south and his gaze would put the spotlight on Tuck. This was an automatic signal for Tuck to abandon any semblance of common sense and go directly into pledge mode.

While under the spell of the Prophet, Friar Tuck would exercise his natural born instincts to talk incessantly, avoid work and find every opportunity to laugh at himself and the antics of the usual suspects. The Soup Lady mentioned that she had noticed the change in Tuck since the Prophet had joined her small group. Other guardians had also commented on his playful nature becoming more demonstrative. Even his determination to be last in line seemed to take on a new zeal. The Groundhog watched and worried about the changelings.

While sitting in the room for eating the Groundhog informed Friar Tuck that he was going to pay a visit to his home. This was not the first time this conversation had come up. In previous discussions Friar had been evasive about where he lived and the availability of his parents. Because he now appeared to becoming possessed, the Groundhog was committed to calling on some greater powers to intervene. Reluctantly, Friar Tuck gave up his address and drew a map to his house, daring the Groundhog to come. That night the Groundhog made the journey to the home of Friar Tuck but could not gain entry because of the fear of his elderly grandmother. He left a message for Tuck's mother to call him.

Two nights later the call came and when she heard of his antics she said that she was "ashamed" of him. She explained that her family was "from the islands," as if to say island people don't act like that. She indicated that none of the behaviors were exhibited at home where he was a loving and most responsible child. The Groundhog shared his concerns about the changes in his behavior, pointing out that in the last three to four weeks the antics had only gotten worse. As they talked Friar picked up another phone and his efforts were quickly discovered and rebuked. Friar's mother promised to speak to him and assured the Prophet that he would see a change.

The next day Friar Tuck asked to have his desk moved away from the Prophet and all the way to the south end of the village where he could be near the Groundhog. Master Poe granted him permission and he was relocated. For the next four days there was a noticeable positive change in his behavior and not once did he vie to be last in line. Every now and then he could sense the unrelenting efforts of the Prophet to take control of his life but he worked hard at not falling under the influence.

The Groundhog marveled at this apparent battle between the Prophet and the parent to influence the behavior of Tuck in school. For four days it seemed like Tuck had been rescued from the edge but his survival was not a certainty. The paradox of the Prophet's ascension from defiance, lethargy and depression to active recruitment was also puzzling and warranting more in depth understanding. As the Groundhog left The Land Set Aside for Learning he reflected on the wisdom of the old adage "Let sleeping dogs lie."

Four Corners

Somewhere outside of the walls of The Land Set Aside for Learning in places where the Councils of the All Knowing meet there is a body of knowledge that suggests that associates in the Village of Poe benefit from working together and experiences in which they can engage each other. From time to time the Groundhog watched Master Poe attempting to allow the associates to engage in these collaborative activities which often seem to test his tolerance level. As a new guardian Master Poe always faced the challenge of closing the gap between the behaviors that he expected from the associates and what he tolerated. Needless to say the gap was more than fairly wide and the usual suspects had a primary mission of widening it.

One afternoon as the Groundhog entered the village he noticed the associates gathered in four small groups that were dispersed in the corners. In looking at the composition of the groups it appeared that some attention must have been given to assigning the Wanderer, the Prophet, Moses, and Friar Tuck to separate groups. Mo Betta and Secret Squirrel were also separated but because of their introverted approaches collaborative groupings would not be threatened by their usual passive participation.

Although the noise level of the village was probably approaching the intolerable level on Master Poe's scanner all of the groups seemed to be engaged in the assignment, all but one that is. In the southeast corner of the village the noise level had risen to such a pitch that it would have been highly unlikely that any constructive work could be taking place. Master Poe had already confronted Moses about sitting in a large bucket, used to hold recess toys, which he had converted into a bassinette. After a few chants Moses reluctantly gave up the bassinette but returned to the corner and took a seat on some outer garments in order to continue acting like a baby to the delight of the other associates.

The group in the southeast corner was composed of Crown Jewel, Marie Antoinette, Moses, Sister Pearlina and Friar Tuck. As the noise level continued to rise from the corner the Groundhog sauntered over to see what the commotion was about. Standing a few feet away in order to observe but not disturb, he could see and hear Moses entertaining Marie Antoinette and Crown Jewel with comments about how "sexy" they were. Each time he mentioned the word the two girls would giggle uncontrollably. Moses asked "What's so funny? I call my mother sexy all the time." But, the girls could not control themselves and Moses was loving every minute of being on center stage.

The calamity in the corner posed quite a dilemma for the Groundhog. He could request Moses to extricate himself in order to have a private conversation about appropriate language and accomplishing the specific assignment. He could ask each of the girls to come and talk with him and thereby remove the adoring audience. Or, he could plant himself in the corner with the associates and by his presence force Moses to be more thoughtful and the girls to be less responsive. But he did nothing and stood there watching Moses perform for the girls with one eye and watch him with the other.

Soon the time allocated for the cooperative learning exercise came to an end and the associates returned to their domiciles. The Groundhog asked Jewel how much work needed to be done and she indicated that they didn't accomplish much because Moses "wouldn't stop playing." Her comments were shared like a very pleasing complaint. She was obviously not as bothered by the lack of progress as the Groundhog.

Later that evening when the Groundhog was alone and replayed the events of the day, his thoughts turned to Jada Pinkett who had unofficially dropped out of her group and contented herself with drawing pictures while the group discussions took place. He thought about Mo Betta who sat alone complaining that his group was ignoring him. He thought about the Wanderer who worked well with his group as long as they allowed him to do whatever he wanted. But most of all he thought about how Moses' antics wasted the time of the four other associates in his group. He resolved to find a way to ensure that the usual suspects would not destroy the educational opportunities that were available in the Village of Poe.

Honor Codes

In the days immediately following the talk with the mother of Friar Tuck the Groundhog noticed the change in Tuck's behavior. Even in those moments when Tuck was on the verge of lapsing into his overly affable self a glance at the Groundhog would remind him of his tenuous status on the home front. At the end of each day Tuck would ask the Groundhog to send word to his mother on how well he was doing. The Groundhog promised to send a note after a week had passed and he had discussed his behavior with the other guardians. Friar appeared to have been exorcised, although keeping his shoes tied and his pants up was a continuous battle that often required marking on a curve.

On the third day of Friar's probation he turned in a book report that he was especially proud. The cover of the report contained a photocopy of the book cover. Tuck shared that his father had helped him with it because he and his mother had not learned how to make copies on their printer. The report itself had only a few rudimentary paragraphs as if it were written in direct response to the required outline which addressed the characters, setting, plot, summary and level of enjoyment. Since Friar never pretended to be a writer the Groundhog didn't give the length of the report much thought and was pleasantly amused that Tuck was so proud of his efforts.

The day after Tuck's submission, the Soup Lady came to the village to conduct a group discussion of the books the associates had read. All of the associates gathered in a wide circle that spread all the way around the village. Each took turns sharing their books and responding to questions about similarities with other books under discussion. Some had read sequels and discussed common characters and events. Jada Pinkett and the Prophet "passed" each time they were asked to contribute. Friar Tuck was very attentive but contributed very little of substance to the discussions. The Groundhog was pleased to see that four days had passed without Tuck falling under the spell of the Prophet.

The fifth and final day of Tuck's probation happened to coincide with the last day of the year and the day of the joyful celebrations. In the morning Master Poe gave the associates a small slip of paper to complete an assignment on the books that they had read. The four sections of the assignment required the associates to identify the major parts of the book that were presented in the book report outline. Friar appeared to be procrastinating getting this assignment done throughout the morning. Since it had to be turned in prior to participating in the joyful celebrations Master Poe had Tuck sit next to his desk to help him focus on the task at hand. Still Tuck could not will himself to put his thoughts on paper.

When the Groundhog entered the village after returning from the room for eating he saw Friar Tuck looking particularly frustrated. When he inquired about the situation, Tuck informed him that he could not remember the parts of the book that he was being asked to report on and that he had returned the book to the book market. He stated that he had read the book "four days ago" and couldn't remember anything.

The Groundhog sat with Tuck for a while and asked him to think about the previous day's discussion and jot down any of the ideas that came to mind. Tuck began to chant and whine beyond the usual pitch of the warriors. Then he requested that Master Poe send an electronic communication to his mother to see if she could intervene. This was certainly an unusual request from someone about to have his probation revoked. Master Poe agreed to send the communiqué. The Groundhog suggested that Tuck at least get something on paper before his mother responded. Tuck agreed, grabbed the paper, turned abruptly and began writing. After a few minutes had passed he stood up with the look of defiance on his face and handed Master Poe the assignment. In each of the four sections he wrote "I don't no" three times.

Friar walked up to Master Poe's computer to see if his mother had responded. She had not. Suddenly the Groundhog realized that in all likelihood Friar Tuck's parents had worked too closely with him on the report in order to get him back on track following the phone call. Their efforts left Friar holding the bag when it came time to discussing the report on the previous day and totally exposed when it was time to write about it. Now on the day of the joyful celebrations and the fifth day of his probation, Friar had to choose between giving his parents' misguided efforts up or looking like he was back in the warriors' embrace. Somehow he was hoping that his mother would come through.

Master Poe did not confront Tuck about why he could not complete the assignment. He was not allowed to participate in the celebration because of his performance. He pleaded with the Groundhog not to send his "I don't no" treatise home because he would be punished and not get anything for the joyful season. The Groundhog informed him that he would give it some thought. Eventually the Groundhog decided to visit his home during the time away from The Land Set Aside for Learning but after the joyful gift giving day. He hoped that this might allow him to leverage this gesture against some future defiance of Friar Tuck. As he left the village he smiled when he thought about how hard Tuck had fought to maintain the honor of his parents.

Party for the Few

On the final day of learning before the time of joyful celebration the streets of The Land Set Aside for Learning turned into a scene from the Last Days and Times. Throughout The Land Set Aside for Learning as the Guardians prepared their villages for the end of year parties those associates that most frequently show up among the usual suspects are notified of their status as non-participants. The unintended consequence of the mass notifications was that rather than having the customary one or two associates in foul moods large numbers of their compadres went into red alert at the same time.

The Groundhog had not experienced the sounds of mass rebellion that seemed to usher from almost every village. Two principalities had been set aside to accommodate the dissidents. The town of the Woman of Many Colors was designated for those associates who had been grossly delinquent in submitting their homework and the Boro of the Tallest Man was the destination for the most troublesome of the usual suspects. No special transportation accommodations had been arranged which meant the bi-ways were full of the non-participants, who were unrestrained in declaring their rights. At almost every street corner you could hear the declaration "We hold these truths to be self-evident...." and, as might be expected, those uninvited guess were committed to their "duty to abolish that government."

In the midst of the preparations the Groundhog noticed the God E.S. hastily moving through the streets of The Land Set Aside for Learning to capture an associate who upon receiving her Notice of Non-participation went into a state of hysterical declaration, asserting her right to party. Despite her best efforts the God E.S. could not console the young associate and within short order her protestation turned into sobs and whaling as she was escorted away.

Later, in the early afternoon, another call went out to the God E.S. This time a young warrior had taken up the chant and began his uncontrollable dance. By the time E.S. arrived the young associate had reached the point of no return and had to be constrained. In the Great Beyond a straight jacket would have been in order but having none E.S. had to call upon her mighty wings. She quickly swooped him up and the two became entwined in an intimate war dance as they made their way to the Room With No Chairs. At times it was not clear who was leading but all of his chants were countered with moans and grunts of compassionate logic and reason.

Once inside the Room With No Chairs the Emperor was summoned and the three of them rocked the walls and shook the foundation of The Land Set Aside for Learning. When the gates to the room finally opened the Groundhog fully expected to find the God E.S. and the Emperor bound and gagged. Miraculously, they had survived. The Emperor emerged and headed directly to his domicile in an apparent state of distress, leaving the God E.S. exhausted, soaking wet, and praying for the days of joyful celebration.

Back in the Village of Poe the usual suspects were being rounded up for escort to the outposts set up for the non-participants. Moses and several others were sent to the Woman of Many Colors and the Groundhog was commissioned to escort the Prophet and the Wanderer to the Boro of the Tallest Man. As they made their way they chanted the familiar tunes and after a short distance the Prophet could hear the sounds from the Room with No Chairs and decided to part company. The Groundhog chose to stay the course with the Wanderer and upon delivering him, headed back to find the Prophet, who was hiding around the bend pretending to be invisible.

Once exposed, the Prophet resumed his chanting;"I don't want to go. Why do I have to go? Why can't I…" Fortunately, for the Groundhog, he reluctantly entered the Boro of the Tallest Man where he immediately assumed his prone position on the floor. The Groundhog left him in the custody of the Tallest Man and returned to the village.

The Party for the Few had begun with special guests, Crown Jewels parents, showing up to lead the festivities. The Jewels organized a bingo game for the two-thirds of the associates who were allowed to attend. The party went on and the absence of the uninvited seemed to go unnoticed. As the Groundhog watched he wondered about the health of the Jewels, Master Poe, the Woman of Many Colors, the Tallest Man, the God E.S., the Village of Poe, The Land Set Aside for Learning and all of those who were not invited. He imagined a day when the parties would be banned. He looked forward to the coming days of joyful celebrations when all of The Land Set Aside for Learning would sleep. And, he remembered the legendary sleigh rider who proclaimed "Merry Christmas to all, and to all a Good Night."

Points of Light

When the Groundhog first came to the Village of Poe he found 24 associates, most of who were or soon to become 10 years of age. The youngest of the associates was the Rock who turned 9 shortly after the Groundhog's arrival. The oldest associate was the Pretender, who had turned 11 shortly before. Being almost completely unaware of the development of ten year olds, the Groundhog often mused about how the youngest and the oldest were the most enlightened of the male associates. Little did he know that the concept of enlightenment took on a whole new meaning and was much more complex than he ever imagined when trying to apply it to the dispositions and behaviors of the associates. As time passed, he slowly grew to see the points of light offered by each as they came to be a community of learners.

One night as the Groundhog slept he slipped into the ocean of dreams and in his dream he was visited by a light inspector from the Powers that Be. The inspector had heard Master Poe's lamentations, the warriors' chants, and the Emperor's screams and was sent to determine why so much heat and so little light were coming from the village. And so, he sat down with the Groundhog and asked him to share what he had discovered about each of the associates during his stay in the village. The Groundhog thought for a moment and then offered the following profiles in courage:

The Rock, who was the youngest, was short in stature but had his share of weight. He was so pretty that his images always portrayed him fairer than all of the females. The associates pointed to him as the best in the village when it came to manipulating numbers. One day he shared with the village the best advice anyone had ever given him, "Always obey the Ten Commandments and Grace will always abide within you." He said it with such sincerity that everyone knew his comments were not to be trifled with. At different times the Rock had been the direct neighbor of the Prophet, Moses, Secret Squirrel and A-Rod. In spite of their growing pains he has never been moved. His humor is displayed in the jokes and games he plays in the room for eating where he often speaks in another tongue with A-Rod. Athletics are not his forte but he would be a "go to" guy on any team because being in his presence seems to help the associates make sense of the world. He is universally praised by guardians and associates without the envy or competition often seen with the males.

The Pretender is the oldest. Like the Rock he is one of the prettiest of the associates. So much so, that he often comments that his images often make him look like a female. His earring does little to suggest otherwise and he is the only male associate in the village who wears one. His clothes have a distinct ethnic flavor with bright colorful stitched designs. This too contributes to his softness. Although he appears to know the language of the Rock and A-Rod he never converses with them in it. He is one of the tallest associates but has not gained any physical matter that would help his pants stay north of the border. He has the ability to be whoever he wants. His quiet demeanor, academic skills and athletic ability make him one of the chosen. His confidence and humor put him at the head of the class with the females. He is the only associate that can legitimately challenge Moses on every level. Master Poe once said that he had hoped the Pretender would assert himself as the leader, rather than Moses, but he seems contented with his place near the top. He's very likeable and rarely has a day in which his conduct diminishes the light of the village. However, he is overly sensitive to reprimands from the guardians and lapses into sulking and withdrawal when admonished. During the course of the year he gradually became a central part of the usual suspects, an association certain to be a detriment to his social and academic development.

June O'Sullivan is one of the most sensitive. She fulfills the adage, "To know her is to love her." She is quiet, unassuming and tiny. Her reserved nature and stature makes her a favorite with the tiniest associates in the village, like Jada and Two. However, Amelia, who would never register as tiny on any scale, is her ace boon coon. Amelia and June are joined at the hip in the Room for Eating and entertain each other with never ending stories. June has a very serious, almost pensive, side and appears almost lost in her thoughts until Amelia comes along. She is one of the few associates that brings her sustenance to the room in a brown bag. More often than not it is composed of carbohydrates that would better be served as deserts. Amelia jokes that the composition is designed to make everyone jealous. On one particularly, deep-in-thought day the Groundhog tried to rescue her with the song "You Bring Me Joy." His rendition seemed to captivate her but she explained to Amelia that she could not sing with him because "He's married." Her presence in the village is full of quiet energy.

Amelia Badilia is the largest female associate in the village and, by reputation, is the most conversant. She is the best friend to June O'Sullivan. The sight of the two of them standing together is testament to the commonality of big and little boxes. She loves to hug when getting her picture taken and since most of the females are so tiny she always seems to engulf them. Everyday Amelia and June consume their sustenance together and as they talk they complete each others' thoughts. This is no easy task for June since Amelia rarely leaves any thought simply hanging. Amelia loves to talk about her mother who is "25% deaf in the left ear and 75% deaf in the right ear, which makes her 100% deaf in both ears." In spite of her questionable physiological logic, Amelia is one of the best associates in working with numbers. Amelia is among the most respectful associates in the village and even though she never misses an opportunity to converse she comes to the village with a sense of purpose and a desire to succeed.

Bobby Kennedy is one of the most mature male associates. He is the only male to be placed on the Homework Honor Roll. Bobby likes to compete for any prize that is offered in the village. More than any associate Bobby always has to hear what the reward is with no uncertainty. In the day to day life in the village Bobby is very quiet and has never demonstrated any behaviors that would bring unwanted attention. He has no really close friends in the village. In the Room for Eating Bobby is one of the most creative associates and has many unique ways of consuming his sustenance. Repeatedly stuffing ziti into the top of a soft stick pretzel and consuming it one bite at a time seems to give him the greatest pleasure. In the yard for play Bobby's favorite pastime is kickball. He's got skills but is not the best. He's got common sense which keeps him in the mix of a game which at times the rules have great flexibility. Laura Engels often chooses him to pitch to her. If he is noticed he would be hard not to like. More than any male associate he seeks help when he needs it and is never to proud to ask. Over time Bobby developed more than a passing interest in being part of the usual suspects. They never embraced him and he never lost his mind long enough to get lost in their shenanigans.

I'm New comes to The Land Set Aside for Learning everyday in pursuit of the purpose for which it was created. He wants to learn. His parents moved into a new home in order for I'm New to be taught in an environment where supposedly more associates were committed to the same goals. This is his first year in The Land Set Aside for Learning and his response to many of the questions about life in the Village of Poe is "I'm new!" He comes with the same determination that can be seen in Bobby Kennedy but his skills are slightly less. By most standards his performances are below average but not failing. Since the new year he spends his days in the domicile next to the Prophet. He has the intestinal fortitude and common sense to be in the midst of the continued destructive antics of the usual suspects but not become a part of it. I'm New's father attended the night for the parents and ensured Master Poe of I'm News orderly behavior. He is a solid citizen and makes the village a better place. He recites none of the warrior's chants and offers a positive warmth that has been lost among the usual suspects.

The Drummer is the largest associate in the village. He is a reader and when left to his own volition chooses to read independently. He's quiet and compassionate. His closest associate is Secret Squirrel and each day they spend most of their "free time" together. Despite, or maybe because of, his size he has no athletic ability. Since Secret Squirrel is the smallest associate the two of them look like the odd couple. When asked to imitate a drummer in a high school marching band, the drummer cleared the floor and did an enthusiastic impersonation of the Radio City Rockettes. His performance suggested that the drum had been left in the car. The associates roared with laughter and after about 2 minutes he was exhausted. The Drummer has a lot of parental support but is not big on getting his homework done. He enjoys attention but usually earns it by calling out the most ridiculous answers to make the associates laugh with rather than at him. He has the potential to become a serious successful student but a lazy disposition.

Secret Squirrel is the smallest associate. He's talented and like his best friend the Drummer he loves to read. He suffers from the separation of his parents and on many days acts out by going under his desk or some secluded place in the village because he misses his mother. Many of his journal entries are about his hatred of school and his father. On his bad days he often speaks of death and going to Hell. Unlike the usual suspects, Secret Squirrel demonstrates little anger. He gets into battles with Master Poe over not completing assignments where he refuses to cooperate. He comes from a Republican family and has many stories about the Democrats that he doesn't like. He has trouble with knowing that the Groundhog is a Democrat because he doesn't "look or talk like one." Secret Squirrel is among the smartest associates in the village. If his psychological scars can be healed he will go far in the Great Beyond but the ongoing pain of being away from his mother certainly impedes his chances.

Jada Pinkett is truly a quiet oddity. She has so much more to offer than she shares in the village where she rarely speaks. She has great difficulty writing and therefore writes as little as possible. In the Room for Eating she comes alive in the company of June O'Sullivan, Marie Antoinette and Amelia Badilia. Jada speaks two languages but only listens, secretly, to A-Rod and the Rock as they speak her father's first language. Her attire suggests that she pretty much dresses herself and her huge head of hair only gets periodic attention. After observing her at the Great Tissue Escape on too many occasions, the Groundhog took her to the Room for Healing so that she could be instructed in the art of emptying her nostrils. Throughout the day she takes ten minute retreats to dab at the accumulated mucus with one tissue after another after another. Her work is rarely completed or even submitted and Master Poe has come to accept her response of "No" to his inquiry regarding whether it was done. Her quiet aloof demeanor makes her a primary candidate for slipping through the proverbial "cracks." Her eating habits are among the worst. Little in the Room for Eating ever gets consumed. One day when June O'Sullivan pointed out that the Groundhog only had six cookies for lunch, Jada, with a very sympathetic face, asked if she could have one. He gave her the cookie with the wrapper and she promptly gave the wrapper back. When asked if she thought it would be appropriate to simply throw it away with her own trash, she smiled as if she understood the error of her ways but would not comment. Jada's light shines bright in the company of the female associates, but she offers very little to the guardians.

The Prophet will probably be the associate that Master Poe will remember most vividly at the end of his journey. When confronted with challenges not to his liking he retreats into the Zone of the Unreachable. His responses to the authority of Master Poe and the Emperor are most frequently defiant. Like the Wanderer he refuses to do anything that was not in his immediate plans. He is one of the most disruptive forces in the village. He likes working with numbers more than anything else and also has artistic abilities. When the challenge of numbers is acceptable to him he can be engaged for long periods of time. However, when he senses failure there is little that can be done to assure him that the task should not be catastrophized. His trigger is very short and once engaged he destroys everything that he encounters. Jeremiah is the closest associate to him, primarily because they have been on the same athletic teams for three years. His athletic skills are average and his response to authority during competition is consistent with what he displays in the village. His mother is concerned about his behavior and academic performance. His father is in denial that anything is not quite right. On most days the Prophet comes to The Land Set Aside for Learning looking hurt and neglected. His clothes are either new or soiled. The Groundhog has developed a relationship with him and during his travels through the village has seen him become easier to be around but his antics and lack of trust are impediments to him accepting assistance with his quest for Father Island. Over the course of the year he was transformed from a reclusive isolationist to one of the most galvanizing forces at the center of the usual suspects.

Jeremiah is one of the biggest associates. He is good natured and very even keeled. He doesn't commit much energy to his work in the village and is more than happy just getting something done. He is the closest friend to the Prophet primarily because he is not offended by his antics. Their relationship is rather one-sided and does not favor Jeremiah. Jeremiah is well behaved but lacks motivation. He is quick to be distracted and become engaged in activities that simply waste his time. He has more than his share of toys that he brings to the village and they serve as ready reminders that there is something more fun than learning. His parents are visible in the village and very interested in his work but seem to tolerate his lack of performance. Eating is one of his favorite pastimes and even though he likes sports his early growth spurt makes him less than nimble. In so many ways he is an average guy just enjoying his time growing up in the Village of Poe. His good nature and personal values enable him to avoid participating with the usual suspects even though the Prophet would be his best friend.

Crown Jewel is "The One." She is the one all of the associates want to sit with, wherever she is sitting. She is the one all of the guardians would like to have in their villages. She is by far the most mature associate. She is conscientious about her work and values good grades. Her closest friend in the village is Winnie the Pooh. Moses has a particular fondness for her and unfortunately when given the opportunity provides more than enough assistance to make her grades like his. Just as Moses is the alpha male, she is the alpha female. On most days Jewel is focused and surrounds herself with like minded associates. She has a great sense of humor and as the saying goes "plays well with others." Without a doubt she shines brighter than all of the lights in the village.

Winnie the Pooh leads by example. When given the opportunity she partners with Crown Jewel and the two of them become "the chosen." Laura Engels once proclaimed with all of the sincerity within her being that "the two of them never do anything wrong." Winnie is bright and mature and in so many ways is probably what Master Poe imagined most of the associates would be like when he began his apprenticeship. She likes to write and share her writing reflections. In the midst of the constant storms and flash fires that take place in the village she remains unshaken. Somehow she comes to the village everyday with a quiet resolve to live the Taoist proverb "Take what you can use and let the rest rot."

Moses is a reluctant leader but his presence has a profound impact on the associates around him. His life has been hard by any standards. His family life has suffered major disruptions on several occasions. Those who brought him into the world are no longer with him. Those who claimed him are no longer together. He is one of the primary disrupters to the education process in the Village of Poe. Although he is physically the most dominant male associate, he is also the most immature and can turn the slightest gesture into a major offense and cause for defiance. He is the master of the warrior chants and with quick order can request escapes to the nurse, the bathroom, to get water, to see Princess Leia or anything or anyone that can get him out of the village. He has reading and numbers skills but his antics keep him from developing them. He can be charming and disarming and hostile and belligerent all within a ten minute period. One on one he is easy to talk to but in a group his insecurity makes him hostile. He seeks the approval of his peers rather than the guardians. Trust is not one of his more endearing qualities and anger is the emotion that he most readily displays. He is at the core of the usual suspects.

The Wanderer is a soloist and would be a challenge to the Master of Masters. Somehow his blue, red and white wires must have gotten mixed with the aqua, purple and yellow ones and what should have been labeled AC functions as an alternating DC current which more often than not sends an oppositional polar charge to his on and off switch. That pretty much explains the instructions on how he operates. Somewhere within his rebellious spirit is a longing for his father, who he says no longer communicates with him because he doesn't want his mother to know his phone number. On most days his primary objective is to show the associates that there is nothing that Master Poe, or the Emperor for that matter, can make him do. This includes the simplest things like going to recess or lunch or getting in line. His command of the 3R's is by far overshadowed by his unwillingness to do anything that he is asked. He is the Master of the Warrior's chants. Even though he is small in stature the out of bounds nature of his spirit and total defiance of authority gives him great intimidating powers with law abiding associates. He likes to talk at the other associates and the conversations are rarely mutual exchanges. Princess Leia says that he is a model client because of his dual personality which is never defiant with her. There was a tremor in the universe when he announced he was leaving The Land Set Aside for Learning. The power surge was completely off the grid. Once gone, no one asked about him.

Laura Engels is full of laughter. She is a model citizen and seems to get along with everyone. In the village her hand goes up at every opportunity to participate and even though her responses sometimes come up short she is always ready with a spontaneous second shot. She is the most athletic female associate and kick ball is her passion. Her kicking skills leave much to be desired but she can catch the line drives with the best of the males and has no reservation about arguing over the fairness of the rulings. In the Room for Eating Laura is engaging with the two sets of females, those that the males pursue and those that seem least interested in the males. She is the daughter of a teacher and one of those associates that come each day with a desire to be there. Her persona brightens the village for everyone.

Mo Betta always seems to have the blues. His normal face says "something is wrong and I'm getting the short end of the stick." Reportedly his early years with his father were less than safe. Somehow he has developed a dependence on Jimmy Dean for constant attention and affirmation. He does not play well with others and the slightest infraction sends him into the corner. His writing and numbers skills are less than. He craves the personal attention that is not available in a village with so many aggressive personalities. If he played baseball, he would be the right fielder standing alone watching the air planes fly by or ants gathering. His melancholic spirit is approachable because it is his way of inviting attention from peers and those in authority. Saying that he is "over sensitive" would be an understatement. Because he wears his emotions on his sleeves he can be easily manipulated. He is among the leaders in those most in need of emotional support and one of the few that is willing to accept it.

Jimmy Dean is one of the brightest and most mature of the male associates. In so many ways he is a model associate. He is outgoing and has great command of the language. He has a reservoir of knowledge beyond what is taught in The Land Set Aside for Learning and as a result answers and raises questions in a most constructive manner. He is the closest friend to Mo Betta even though he clearly does not care for the dependence. He is neither athlete nor intellect. All of the associates seem to like him. He rarely has bad days and seems to enjoy being in the village but clearly is not interested in being great. He is the male associate most likely to raise his hand and respond to questions from Master Poe. He is the associate who would be voted Most Likely to Succeed and the least likely to seek the recognition.

Marie Antoinette is a model citizen. Wherever Marie sits she makes her neighbor a little better. Admittedly, A-Rod chose not to want to sit next to her because she reportedly thought she was too smart to answer his questions. And, when given control of the pencil sharpener for her group her patience was quickly worn thin and she created a most restrictive list of times that she would be sharpening pencils. Still, she knows the purpose for coming to school and makes the most of it without complaint, except when her mother doesn't sign her homework. Marie Antoinette comes from a large multi-generational household of twelve with an aunt and uncle also attending The Land Set Aside for Learning. She is one of the best eaters in the village and one of the few that selects raw vegetables as the main entrée in the Room for Eating. Marie seems to be a friend to all but best friends with none. She presented the Groundhog with a BFF bracelet and checked that he was wearing it the next few days. She seeks out the Groundhog's company in the Room for Eating and often shares stories about her father who is away fighting in a war and won't be her father much longer and the boyfriend of her mother who is going to become her father. Most of the associates treat her as one of the brightest bulbs in the pack.

Friar Tuck lives in the fantasy of a father who he believes to be a "gangsta entrepreneur." Tuck is larger than most of the associates and his girth is also seen in his tongue which gives him the look of the legendary Baby Huey. He is handsome and the sparkle in his dark eyes reflects the goodness in his heart. He slowly mastered the art of donning the façade of oppositional defiance and disrespect which he does to gain the favor of the usual suspects. Even when he feigns to be angry he has a difficult time holding back a smile when his anger is mocked. Friar is one of the six "Title" associates that are instructed once a day by the Soup Lady. In the presence of the Prophet and Moses, Friar can easily be converted into a foil for their antics. He is an affable follower who struggles with valuing the approval of his peers over the guardians. It is easy to like Tuck because he wants to do well and be accepted by everyone. He is the youngest in his family and appears to have been treated as such a little too long. He does the minimum amount of work, gives the minimum effort and expects to be rewarded simply because he is there. Although he practices the warrior's chants more often than not it sounds like whining. More than any associate his relationship with the usual suspects changed him into a not so likable associate. If Moses and the Prophet were "Mo and Larry" he would certainly be "Curly."

Sister Pearlina is one of the most easygoing associate. She believes in justice and defends the weak. She often expresses sentiments that suggest she wants Master Poe to "finally get mad" at the usual suspects. Pearlina is a social being who models good behavior but has to be constantly reminded to stay on task. When asked about her mediocre work she sighs, puts her arm on the Groundhog's shoulder and explains her plans to do better next week. She gets along with everyone. Before the Rabbit left the village she was the closest associate to him and they spent their days playing little tricks on each other. When Jeremiah asked if he could have one of her chicken nuggets, after eating two orders of his own, she quickly licked all of them and offered them to him with a big smile. She openly likes the village and wants to be of service to Master Poe. The Land Set Aside for Learning is the place she wants to be even though getting good grades is more of a passing fancy than a commitment.

A-Rod has a sweet spirit. He often skirts around the zone with the usual suspects but has an internal alarm that goes off before he gets in too deep. At that point he becomes apologetic. He is from the Big Apple and is most proud of the fact that on his tenth birthday President Obama was inaugurated and his mother took him to D.C. to see him. A-Rod says that his father was a police officer back in the Big Apple and does not allow him to speak English at home. He and the Rock often engage in their at-home language when they discuss their favorite television shows. For some reason they never include the Pretender and Jada Pinkett in their sidebars even though Jada informs them that she knows what they are saying. A-Rod's writing and numbers work are less than they should be. One day he informed the Groundhog that he no longer wanted to be a part of a cluster because Marie Antoinette thought that she was too smart to answer his questions. He is easily influenced by others and with more structure could become a much brighter light than he has shown.

Two of a Kind is the sweetest of the associates. On most days her voice is barely audible, so much so that the Groundhog often fears he has suffered a hearing loss when talking with her. She has the distinction of having a sister who came from the same egg. When they travel to each other's room for numbers they leave notes. Two says the only way she can distinguish herself in a picture with her sister is that she always wears pink and her sister wears lavender. They have necklaces of the corresponding colors to help others make the distinction. Two is serious about her work and in spite of her diminutive stature will become outspoken with any of the usual suspects that disrupt the small groups that she is assigned to work in. One of her favorite entrees in the Room for Eating is pizza with Ranch salad dressing. She wants to be with Winnie and Jewel even though they relegate her to a second class status.

The Rabbit was probably the most impetuous of all of the associates. For some unknown reason he had the habit of moving quietly through the village and tossing the possessions of other associates on the ground when they were not looking. These acts of looting seemed to be random with no particular motivation. When questioned about his behavior, the Rabbit simply shrugged and put his head down. The Rabbit and the Prophet found it impossible to stay away from each other and when they were together there was never a peaceful moment. Whether in the Room of the Woman of Many Colors, or the Book Market, or the Room for Eating, or roaming through the streets of the Village, the two of them would come together like opposite winds and create the most tumultuous storms. On the other hand, Sister Pearlina and the Rabbit did very well together. Each time they passed each other's domicile they would pay the other back by disturbing some personal possession. Pearlina seemed to understand that it was just his way. There were rumors that the mother of the Rabbit was not pleased with his plight in the Village of Poe and had requested he be put into the witness protection program and relocated. Initially the Emperor and Lt. Uhora were opposed to her demands but after continued instances of random acts of terror, Master Poe was supportive of the move and the Rabbit was no longer a citizen of the village. Every now and then he is spotted in the Room for Eating and Sister Pearlina and Laura Engels make a big deal out of waving to him. Moses and the Prophet have to be continuously reminded of the restraining order.

Having heard the various accounts of the lives of the associates the inspector gave the Groundhog a very puzzled look. Slowly she put away her notebook and pulled out a book that had been given to her by My Favorite Martian. It was entitled No Place Like Home." As she searched for a place in the book she explained how the associates received their initial wiring prior to coming to The Land Set Aside for Learning and that many of the factors impacting on the quality of the wiring are beyond the control of the guardians. She said it was important to understand that the anecdotes about the lives of the associates provided insight into the disparity of the workmanship and the challenges faced by Master Poe.

Once she found the bookmark that she had been searching, she asked the Groundhog to come closer so that she could talk with him in private. She shared that Master Poe had a noble charge to create a second home for the associates where he would be a single parent. She said this was codified in the Latin term "in loco parentis" which meant to act like a parent. In this second home the wiring of the associates could potentially be rerouted in the hopes that they would all shine brighter in 24 points of light.

The light inspector read on, sharing the four building blocks needed in the second home for it to be effective. The first was the installation of a sense of "belonging." In order to develop the maximum capacity of the associates it was vital that they feel they are an integral part of the family of Poe. Their place in the village had to be secure and their value to Master Poe and to each other had to be continuously reinforced. Those who came with Pooh connections from their first home, like the Prophet, Moses and A-Rod, would have difficulty feeling connected. A total makeover might be needed and hard to accomplish in the short time they spent in the village.

The second building block that she pointed out was "power." This she said was the ability of the associates to make choices that affected the outcomes of their daily efforts. When the associates could see that they could influence the world around them they would also be able to create a comfortable productive place for themselves within it. Associates whose wiring was set to help them survive in unstable environments would feel powerless and not prepared to operate in the new setting.

The third building block was "freedom." She explained that freedom was the ability to make choices about the things that matter. This was a block that rested on the ability of Master Poe to set high expectations as well as limits for what could happen in the village. Without freedom the associates would not feel the power to have ownership of their activities. Many of the associates had come into the village from places where freedom had been denied because of too much structure or the total lack of structure which ultimately allowed for wasted energy.

The fourth and final building block needed to ensure the success of the associates was "fun." She pointed out that fun is the inevitable result of the other three blocks being put into place. Like with freedom, Master Poe was pivotal. If the interaction in the village was fun for him, than it would be fun for everyone. Fun had to be developed in the small everyday things like morning greetings, everyday celebrations and birthdays and holidays, as well as more formal learning opportunities. She whispered, "The most crucial person in all of this is Master Poe. If he is having fun, the associates will usually be having fun. If he can laugh out loud, the associates can laugh out loud. If he can be spontaneous, the associates can be spontaneous."

The Groundhog thanked the light inspector for her insights on belonging, power, freedom and fun. He told her that he would continue to reflect on her advice as he worked to improve the points of light coming from the village and promote the development of a second home for the associates.

Unhappy Hour

Everyday six of the usual suspects go to the Inn of the Soup Lady for the better part of an hour. The Groundhog noticed that the absence of the six from the village made it a most pleasant place. However, when the associates returned to the village it was like a huge cloud of smoke descended, drastically changing the climate. Usually the Soup Lady accompanied the associates on their return and more often than not her expressions suggested that she had experienced another unhappy hour.

The Soup Lady's spirit was being warn down by the encounters with the associates and she often shared her concerns about how the composition and dynamics of the group had been altered by the addition of the Prophet. Apparently his presence was like an intoxicant to Moses and Friar Tuck, causing them to become rebellious and disrespectful. Each day when the group met, new and less productive patterns of behavior were becoming part of the modus operandi.

The Groundhog asked her if she felt his presence might help sober up the associates. She turned down his offer, saying that she had a couple of strategies that she was working on. A few weeks passed with the usual stories of insobriety at the Inn. Then on the day before the joyful celebrations the Soup Lady brought the usual suspects together for the customary unhappy hour. Because it was the end of the year she had decided to give them a "reward" for the progress they had made and to commemorate the less than memorable time they had shared. The Soup Lady was obviously a very forgiving guardian who believed in the adages "Whatever doesn't kill you will blind you." and "If you turn a blind eye it won't be there." This seemed to work in the 5PM happy hours in the Great Beyond but as a discipline philosophy in The Land Set Aside for Learning was still being tested.

She gathered the associates around her table and spoke to them about how far they had come and some of the challenges of the coming year. Much to her dismay, the Prophet, not being one to talk about the future, interrupted her, hoping to fast forward to the gifts that she had assembled and avoid the possibility of being dismissed based on future expectations. After several exchanges she confirmed his prophecy and asked him to leave the Inn. When he refused after several exchanges she sent for the Groundhog who was just down the street.

When the Groundhog entered the Inn the Prophet was looking more forlorn than ever. The sounds of parties for the few were in the air, his notice of non-participation was expected at any moment and the gifts on the table were quickly becoming out of reach. In a moment of desperation and panic he grabbed a gift from the table and taunted the Soup Lady with it. The Groundhog escorted him out of the Inn at which time he threw the gift away stating he didn't want it anyway. The Soup Lady stated that because of the holiday, he should be forgiven. The Groundhog suggested that perhaps a quiet execution would be a more effective remedy.

The series of events convinced the Groundhog to pay a visit to the Inn of the Soup Lady during the unhappy hour the first week of the new year. Upon entering the inn he found the Soup Lady seated at a half-circle table with the six associates seated around the outside. Positioned clockwise, beginning on her left were Moses, Friar Tuck, Mo Betta, Jada Pinkett, the Prophet and A-Rod. The Groundhog placed himself at an adjacent table where he could observe the interaction of the associates. Throughout the unhappy hour Moses and the Prophet engaged in a continuous series of disruptive antics consisting of verbal and non-verbal exchanges only remotely related to the lesson. A-Rod and Friar Tuck added their mindless chatter in order to be included in the distracting frivolity. Mo Betta retreated from the table, placing himself against the nearest wall and donned his "I'm hurt" façade. Jada Pinkett rocked back and forth as if she were trying not to fall asleep.

As the Groundhog watched he noticed each of the associates watching him, watching them, watching him. To each he gave any eye of disapproval and each responded with a look of embarrassment while continuing their waywardness. When it finally ended the Soup Lady and Groundhog talked about the wasted time and minimum progress being made. He suggested that the two incendiary forces be split up and each alternate being in the Inn every other day. The other could be instructed outside of the Inn in a makeshift half-way house under the watchful eye of the Groundhog. The Soup Lady indicated that this would require a "major roster change." Her response suggested a commitment to the continued abuse and the Groundhog offered no other alternatives.

It was obvious that the associates and the Soup Lady were locked in a battle with the unintended consequences being her sense of ownership and the stigma attached to them being identified by Master Poe as "The Soup Lady's group." Just as it was in the Great Beyond, those who spent too much time at the Inn carried the stigma. The act of getting help and the image of being in need of help was not one embraced by the usual suspects. And so it was that each day an unhappy hour was spent with the Soup Lady making offerings to the six most in need but living in oppositional defiance.

Boys on a Raft

One day when Master Poe had scattered the associates in small groups around the village the Groundhog took a leisurely stroll to see how they were faring. The first stop he made was where Bobby Kennedy, the Prophet and the Pretender were gathered. As he approached he thought about how a more unlikely trio could not have been put together. He could see Bobby Kennedy lying prone, supported on his shoulders making his deliberate etchings on his paper. It had always fascinated the Groundhog to see how Bobby held his pencil in his left hand with the thumb tucked under the fingers as if he were applying a death grip.

The Prophet was also on the ground but appeared to be hiding from the view of the Groundhog. Even though his paper was out he was committing the usual minimal amount of effort to getting anything on it. Above the two of them stood the Pretender, looking as if he was getting ready but uncertain about where he fit into the cramped quarters they had staked out. The sight of the three of them conjured up the image of Huck Finn and two runaways heading down the Mississippi.

The Groundhog took a seat next to the associates and inquired about their progress on the assignment. Never one to miss an opportunity to be rude, the Prophet responded from beneath the table by repeating each question in a mocking manner. Bobby Kennedy attempted to explain the assignment over the Prophet's mocking. The Pretender, who could have been a stabilizing force, stood by and laughed at the continued comments from the Prophet.

Master Poe overheard the Pretender laughing and suggested that he stop and get to work. Hearing this as an unfair reprimand he immediately went into his version of the warrior's chant, jerking his shoulders and poking out his lips, already red and swollen from the cold. In a more stern voice Master Poe implored him not to imitate the behaviors of the usual suspects and try to focus on the assignment. The Groundhog reinforced the sentiment as the Pretender looked off with his arms folded in defiance.

In trying to turn the attention back to the assignment the Groundhog asked how far they had gotten. Bobby Kennedy sensing that they were adrift without a rudder, continued to write without looking up. The Prophet continued his performance of repeating the questions and hiding out. The Pretender was caught between trying to get back on track and reinforcing the Prophet's antics. The combination of impulses displayed by the three assured only one thing that in the absence of some form of intervention the raft that they were on was going nowhere with no direction.

The Groundhog moved away, sensing that his presence had become the stage for the Prophet's performance. Taking a position a little further down the road he watched from the short distance and came to see how the promise of the three was analogous to the promise of the diversity in the Great Beyond. Bobby Kennedy was from the North and came to the village everyday with a desire to develop his tools. He sought help when he needed it and in so many ways epitomized the ideal of not seeing things that are and asking why but dreaming of things that could be and asking why not. The Pretender was from a place where another language was more natural and yet he mastered the language of the village as well as any of the associates. In part due to his age and family life in the Great Beyond he was more mature than most male associates and had a strong sense of right and wrong. His occasional alliances with the usual suspects were always fleeting and his leadership potential always brought them to him. In so many ways he could be a force for positive change but the lure of the usual suspects was appealing to him.

The Prophet was from the South and his troubled history kept the promise of his prophecy in constant peril. Most of his days were spent in quiet desperation while he created ways to keep those who cared about him at a distance. His eyes suggested a deep seated hurt and his behavior more often than not was reflective of a wounded creature trying to avoid more pain. Indeed he had developed the skills needed to be in perpetual motion and go nowhere. His life reinforced the understanding that those who need love the most are often the least lovable.

As the Groundhog watched he became more determined to find a way to break through the defenses of the Prophet who in so many ways was "the least of these." For the moment the raft would have to continue making its way pushed only by the unforgiving motion of time. Later that evening he made his way to a basketball in order to support the Prophet in a different setting. After waiting an hour, the result of having been given the wrong time by Jeremiah, the game began. Midway through the first quarter the Prophet entered the game with his team down 10-2. In the next three minutes the life of the Prophet in the Village of Poe was played out on the basketball floor.

Like most of the associates in the league, the Prophet played the game with a high level of anxiety due to the pressure of the parents who sat on the sidelines shouting a constant stream of directions. His single-minded mission was to bring the team back, which most simply put meant "just shoot it." The first time he touched the ball he scored a basket. The second time he touched the ball he was fouled and this infraction led to him pushing the offender. In the third play that he was involved in he fouled the shooter and the two of them fell to the floor. As they got up and the shooter walked to the foul line, the Prophet hit him in the back of the head with the ball. After the free throws were taken the Prophet's team took the ball out and as luck would have it the Prophet headed up the court with the ball, resuming his mission. Again, he was defended by the same player. This time the play ended up in a jump ball as the two fell to the floor scrambling for control. When the whistle blew so did the Prophet. He began punching the defender. For his actions he was immediately ejected from the game, having played less than three minutes.

As the Groundhog watched the series of plays unfold in stunned silence tears began to overcome his spirit. He imagined how much pressure the Prophet must have felt watching his team fall behind so quickly. He wondered why no one in authority had seen and addressed all of the small infractions which happened so unexpectedly and led to the final outbreak. He watched the father of the Prophet, dressed in his public enemy outfit, go across the court to admonish the Prophet for losing control. He worried that this game was part of the prophecy for the life of the Prophet. He saw the Prophet slowly moving his seat on the bench behind the others as he retreated into the Zone of the Unreachable while his four year old brother looked on, another portent of things to come.

The following day the Groundhog paid a visit to the Prophet to see if there were noticeable effects from the game. Not surprising, he was his old self, picking up his usual mocking mode from the previous day. The Groundhog decided not to engage him in a conversation about the game but rather to check on his work. He asked if he could be of help and the Prophet ensured him that he needed no help. Since it was apparent that he had not written more than two not so neat lines on his paper the Groundhog persisted. The Prophet continued his line of defense that help was not needed. Feeling frustrated by the tactics, the Groundhog suggested that he did not have to be afraid to admit he needed help because that was his purpose for being there. The Prophet's response to the suggestion that he might be afraid was that "The only person I'm afraid of is God." The Groundhog smiled and thought that God would certainly have to be brought in to pull the Prophet from the raft that he had isolated himself on. He slowly moved away while offering a silent prayer that God somehow would let him be the rope.

Happier New Year

When the Groundhog returned to the village after the Days of Joyful Celebrations he discovered that Master Poe had completed a total relocation of the domiciles. This was the fourth reconstruction effort since his first visit. Master Poe shared that in the beginning he had organized the associates into small clusters of four and five. That arrangement did not work well because many of the associates became engaged in continuous sidebars as they got to know each other rather than focusing on his instruction.

The first reconstruction effort forced the associates into the now famous horseshoe configuration with 18 domiciles forming the perimeter and six placed in opposing directions in the center. The advantage of the configuration was that Master Poe could command the attention of the associates while standing at the open end. The disadvantage was that associates that became distractions could quickly become center stage and perform for the entire village at any moment.

Having developed a better understanding of the dynamics of the associates' interaction, Master Poe relocated them into linear clusters of three and four with everyone facing the north end of the village where he most commonly stood. The next configuration found the associates paired in twos and lined into three columns facing north. Then on the day that groundhogs are watched most closely without shootings the associates were organized into small u-shaped clusters of four with the open ends facing north.

While walking around the village the Groundhog mused over how the continuous changes of the domiciles was in such contrast to by-gone days when they were permanently fastened to the ground in straight rows, all facing north, where an associate had a place and at a moments glance could be detected as absent. Everything seemed to have a place then and relationships were imbedded into memories because of who sat in front or behind him or in the front or the back of the village. There was a place for the good and the bad and visitors to the villages knew something about you based on your location. Like so many things in the Great Beyond the stability of what was had been replaced by a commitment to constant change.

A new day was also in store for the monitoring of the behavior of the associates. Mind Reader had created a "Group" of approximately six associates from throughout The Land Set Aside for Learning who met periodically to discuss their behavior and other secret stuff. Mind Reader had shared with the Groundhog that in the second half of the year her workload became heavier because many of the guardians had exhausted all of their behavior control procedures and sensed that it was time to bring in someone with her special talents.

Master Poe had also adopted a new strategy to control the activities of the associates by developing a village reward system, "Poe's Pennies," based on a "banking system" with paper currency of assorted denominations with his picture on them. Like in the Great Beyond there were denominations of five, ten, twenty, fifty and one hundred dollars. Each week the currency could be earned or lost based on a prescribed set of behaviors. Master Poe established four primary rules: 1) Always be prepared for class. 2) Raise your hand when you have something to contribute or a question. 3) Be considerate of your classmates. 4) Follow directions the first time they are given. Indeed these rules would be equivalent to establishing a new world order in the Village of Poe. The Groundhog feared the coming of an army of recorders to enforce the new deal. How else could these activities be tracked while the Master was teaching.

Master Poe provided the associates with a list of behaviors that would guide them in gaining or losing specific amounts of the currency: 1) No homework $50. 2) No raising hand $20. 3) Not working $20. 4) Talking in Streets $200. 5) Messy desk/area $50. 6) Disrespecting the guardians $100. 7) Being unprepared $50. 8) Discipline outside the village $100. Every nine weeks Master Poe would hold an auction of various goods and prizes where associates could bid on things like – computer time $50, ping pong $50, homework pass $100 and lunch in the village $50. Additionally, Master Poe established "jobs" that associates could be "given" without pay: Treasurer (1), Assistant Treasurer (1), Teller (4), Collector (3), and Secret Reporter (2). The most intriguing was the Secret Reporters, known only to Master Poe, who were responsible for observing behavior outside of the classroom.

The Groundhog inquired about the thinking behind the banking system and was informed that it was recommended by Mind Reader and another guardian who served as Master Poe's "mentor." As he listened to Master Poe review the two pages of instructions and watched the responses of the associates he began to wonder about the largest identified penalty being for "Talking in the streets." He remembered how important it was for the guardians to continually remind the associates not to talk as they moved from village to village throughout the day. Despite the "no talking" rules and walking in a "straight line on the second square" ordinance, the associates seemed predestined to violate both of these requirements. Some of the older guardians had changed from a complete prohibition to a continuous plea of permissive conversation in lower decibels. This seemed to work but $200 for talking in the street and $100 for disrespecting the guardians seemed somewhat disproportionate.

The usual suspects had more than their share of questions about the banking system. They posed their concerns in ways that suggested three of the four primary rules on raising your hand, being considerate, and following directions on the first time, were totally foreign to them. Surprisingly, none of them requested consideration for the job of the "Secret Reporter." As they sorted out their issues for clarification the Groundhog began to think about the consequence of not having any currency to pay for the $50 weekly rental fee for each domicile or when the penalties exceeded the usual suspects' ability to pay. Certainly, being expelled from the village or maybe "shunned" for a month would be the best penalty.

Just keeping up with the new location of the domiciles and new rules of order kept the Groundhog's mind churning and undoubtedly would do the same for Master Poe. If tracking the daily behavior of the Prophet for Mind Reader seemed like a fulltime job the new order of things to come would be as demanding as understanding the national economic stimulus package. Yes, there was a new order and with it came more demands that would come at a high cost to the village. The "group meetings" would bring together the leading usual suspects from throughout The Land Set Aside for Learning. This new group identity, like being one of the "Soup Lady's group," could create a new sense of belonging or further alienation.

The Groundhog had always feared creating a formal group of the usual suspects within the Village of Poe because this imposed identity could make them different, a possible subculture within the village. Despite his reluctance, forces throughout The Land Set Aside for Learning were repeatedly molding the usual suspects into a common identity. In his way of thinking the key to their rehabilitation was to reach them as individuals detached from the suspects that they were most comfortable. He remembered the old days in the Great Beyond when groups were called gangs and the authorities met periodically with them to talk about the consequences of their ways. He feared that the young associates would respond to the reason and logic of the meetings with increased opportunities to perform and demonstrate their defiance as they built upon their alienation within their villages.

As new relationships developed based on the relocation of the domiciles he worried that new recruits like Friar Tuck and A-Rod who needed stability might stray further from Master Poe, and that they would engage in behaviors that communicated their precarious unity with Moses and the Prophet. Somehow a banking system with play money to reward the behaviors of associates whom the bar had been set so low was going to lead to a lot of uncollectable debt and ultimately bankruptcy and possible looting. Like the lessons observed in the Great Beyond, the gap between the haves and the have nots was only going to become greater.

The Cavalry

On the day following the charting of winter by the behavior of the groundhogs the Soup Lady came into the village looking more befuddled than usual to report that the Prophet had departed the unhappy hour without authorization. His whereabouts were unknown and therefore she felt compelled to have the court of the Emperor sound the alarm throughout The Land Set Aside for Learning requesting that he surrender immediately by turning himself in at the Village of Poe. The Groundhog, knowing his hangouts, sought him out in the Room for Human Waste. Within minutes the two of them returned to the village as the alarm was being sounded. The Soup Lady quickly informed the court that indeed the Prophet had returned. She admonished him as she left the village and shared that there would be a consequence.

While standing at the gate of the village, the Prophet began to sink behind a domicile and slowly pulled it into the entrance way. The Groundhog spoke to him about his choices. The Prophet continued in his reconstruction effort while looking lost and hurt. As he talked he mentioned his desire to see the Prophet entering the medical profession. He shared that masters of medicine could not do their work when they are angry. He posed the challenge to the Prophet to let his anger go and get on with his day. But the Prophet was too lost in his pain to let it go and join the rest of the Village.

Soon the associates were coming out of the village on their way to the room of scientific discovery. Master Poe was in the lead and somehow Friar Tuck had managed to find his way back to the end of the line. As they filed past, the Prophet did not look at them but instead stared at the ground between himself and the Groundhog. Only one associate acknowledged his presence at the gate. As might be expected, it was his friend Jeremiah who reached out and called him by name, waving as he passed. The Prophet did not respond. Soon they were gone and it was too late to join them without a display of desire. The Groundhog continued to talk to him about his choices, his anger and his future.

Momentarily, Master Poe returned from his escort duties. He took a position inside the gateway just about five feet behind where the Prophet was standing. From this position he could hear the exchange while remaining out of view. The Prophet sensed his presence and withdrew further, giving the Groundhog less and less eye contact. Sensing that the Prophet was now caught in the dilemma of giving into him or appearing tough for Master Poe, the Groundhog decided to move along offering the Prophet to follow him to the Room of Scientific Discovery. He chose to remain at the entrance to the village.

The Groundhog walked slowly to the room looking back periodically. By the time he reached the room he could see the Prophet and one of the guardians coming in the distance. He was moving at his usual reluctant pace and rubbing his shoulders against the walls of The Land Set Aside for Learning. As the Groundhog watched he noticed that coming behind them was Lt. Uhora, Mind Reader and a uniformed police officer from the neighboring fortress. They quickly overtook the two and Lt. Uhora began an exhortation about his unacceptable behavior. Now Uhora was in her performance mode while Mind Reader and the officer looked on. Little did she know that the Prophet had informed the Groundhog that the only person he was afraid of was God. The three authority figures gave the Prophet a more daunting stage to prove himself by performing his defiant act. It would not be long before he would seek retribution from the Soup Lady, who in his mind would have caused this confrontation. As they proceeded the Groundhog welled up with sadness knowing that the Prophet would not be defeated but still caught up in a battle of wills that could have been avoided.

Upon arriving at the Room of Scientific Discovery the three circled the wagons as Lt. Uhora ordered him into the room. He slowly entered but was in no condition to learn. The Groundhog watched the events unfold from a distance and prayed that one day the Prophet would be able to find peace in the battle between the core value system being authored by his father that said he was a "man" and had to be "hard, tough and strong" and the core of his being that was "soft, resilient and fragile." Every encounter seemed to be full of challenges whether it was with peers or guardians and the home life of the Prophet was unimaginable.

Soon the associates returned to the village. The Prophet went to his domicile and quietly immersed himself in his work while the other associates engaged in their usual antics. For the remainder of the morning he was more subdued than usual, most likely pondering the consequence of another detention or possible arrest. This would be his second detention in as many weeks which would mean his mother would have to bring him to The Land Set Aside for Learning an hour earlier than usual. Having experienced more than his share of detentions his track record suggested that this inconvenience was more than his mother could bear so more often than not he arrived at the detention 20 minutes late.

When it came time to travel to the Room for Eating the Prophet quietly made his way into the line with the other associates. Once in the room he found his space between Moses and Friar Tuck. In no time their energy recharged his battery and the three of them were back to their normal antics of laughing at the associates from the neighboring villages. The Groundhog took a seat in close proximity hoping to talk them into a more sober sense of being. Unfortunately the combination of the three rarely lent itself to pre-pubescent sobriety. As he watched he imagined them to be the infamous "Three Stooges." Moses would undoubtedly be Mo, the Prophet was Larry, and Friar Tuck would have been Curly. He fantasized the three of them being escorted by the cavalry into the back of the short bus and being driven down a cobblestone road into a future of limited possibilities on Father Island where their laughter sounded more like crying.

Snow Days

When the storm finally passed and the roads to The Land Set Aside for Learning were safe to travel the associates returned to the village. The Groundhog had considered extending the two day stay at home to a third day in anticipation of the possible chaos from the hiatus. However, when he entered the village all of the associates were quietly working in their domiciles. Their silence was as eerie as the silence often heard in the early morning hours of an overnight snow storm. No one was moving or talking above a whisper. Master Poe had gathered a small group around him at the south end.

When moving through the village it was apparent that Moses, Friar Tuck, A-Rod and Jada Pinkett were away at the unhappy hour. The Prophet had been relocated to the south end of the village in complete isolation of the six newly developed clusters of associates. Not so surprising, because of his asocial disposition, the Prophet seemed quite contented living in isolation of the others and in close proximity to the Groundhog's hideout.

Throughout the morning Master Poe guided the associates through a series of independent catch-up activities because the normal routine had been disrupted by the two hour delay. Many of the associates worked on poems expressing their love for someone special in their lives. In two days they would celebrate the holiday set aside for sharing these feelings of affection. The Pretender asked for assistance in composing a poem for his mother. He shared that it was easier to just sign a card where someone else had already done the writing. This special holiday and the recent snow storm seemed to have had a very calming affect on everyone.

In the afternoon festivities were held in all the villages and boroughs around The Land Set Aside for Learning. Parents of the associates brought cards and games and refreshments. The Groundhog had not witnessed a celebration of this magnitude since the Parties for the Few. He began to worry that a similar commotion might soon arise but it never did. Everyone seemed contented to share their cards and other tokens of affection. Soon the mother of the Drummer and of the Prophet arrived and began the local celebration by giving out trinkets to play with and make cards. Even though the noise rose to a level shattering the peace of the morning all seemed well throughout the village.

Near the end of the celebration Marie Antoinette presented the Groundhog with a lollipop and sticker. The Prophet, watching from the distance, slowly pulled out a lollipop and offered it to the Groundhog. When the Groundhog realized this show of affection he thanked the Prophet and proclaimed him to be "the best." In keeping with his oppositional posture he assured the Groundhog that "I'm not the best." The Groundhog insisted and the Prophet persisted in his denial. One thing that was undeniable was the smile of embarrassment on the Prophet's face as he shook his head denying his affection for the Groundhog and his status as not the best. The Groundhog just sat in the warmth of his smile hoping for more snow days.

When it came time to leave the village at the end of the day the Groundhog took advantage of this ever so slightly opened window of opportunity and thanked the Prophet again. It seemed like the moment had passed since the only response he could muster was a "No, thank you Miss Groundhog." Still, on this day set aside for cutting out red hearts and giving candy and cards, the Groundhog knew that somewhere in the soul of the Prophet he had earned an ever so tiny space where the Prophet did not have to act so hard. A place where he could care and take the ultimate risk of showing that he was not as hard as the men on Father Isle. Somehow in the days to come the Prophet would have to grow into that space and expand it into his total being. The Groundhog left The Land Set Aside for Learning at the end of the day reflecting on his understanding that this was the reason he had come to the Village of Poe.

Dragons and Drones

When the Groundhog undertook the journey to the river to meet the father of the Prophet, he did so with the intent of expanding the village that nurtured the Prophet. He hoped to construct a more secure bridge between the Prophet's life in the castle in the Great Beyond and his life in the Village of Poe. Upon meeting the father he quickly came to understand that he had come to the meeting to show the Groundhog that he was willing to battle anyone in order to demonstrate that he was a man and that his son was too. This manhood struggle was a constant theme in their discussion and resonated in subsequent encounters with the Prophet when he would proclaim that he was not afraid of anyone but God.

Later when the Groundhog went to the castle of Friar Tuck to meet his father, he did so with the intent of reinforcing the village that nurtured him. Having spoken with the mother and seen only momentary positive change he reached out to the father who was so revered by Tuck as "a gangsta entrepreneur." However, the father was unwilling to engage the Groundhog in a conversation about saving his son's life. Instead, he suggested that all future discussions be channeled through Friar Tuck's mother.

The Groundhog could see that the two of them were representative of the dragons that inhabit the castles where associates in search of Father Isle reside. They are as challenging to understand as their offspring. The demands on their lives and the legacy of their fathers have made some of them hard and left too many of them broken and in fear. Their quest for success in the Great Beyond at times seems as futile and elusive as success for their sons in the Village of Poe.

Following the celebration of cheerful giving The Land Set Aside for Learning responded to the widespread search for Father Isle with the deployment of Drones, a special task force on behavior modification. Under the guidance of the "Behaviorist" Mind Reader debriefing sessions were established on an ongoing basis with "group" participants sharing their progress in the villages. Group membership was based on the level of defiance that had been registered during the first half of the year. These associates were like the all stars of The Land Set Aside for Learning who never get invited to the parties for the few. All of the guardians with responsibilities for the group participants were required to rate them throughout the day on a three point scale. This rating system was designed to provide continuous progress monitoring of the associates.

From the distance the Drones appeared to work towards changing behaviors independent of the cause. Since many of the causes had to be traced to the castles outside the walls of The Land Set Aside for Learning and beyond the flight of the Drones, the focus was on the events that took place upon arrival. The approach seemed to parallel the operation of the drones in the undeclared war in the Great Beyond where from the distance enemies could be spotted and eliminated without direct contact or in depth understanding of the interactions on the ground.

Strategically placed between the Dragons and Drones were the guardians who teach, soldiering each day with their boots on the ground laboring to make sense out of the lives of the Prophet, Friar Tuck and Moses, et al, in order to transform them into good citizens. With varying levels of support and frequent interference from the Dragons and Drones Master Poe fought the odds of turning the usual suspects into more productive associates capable of contributing to the Village and society in the Great Beyond. Through banking systems and rating scales the Drones sent down edicts for him and the other guardians to incorporate into their already over demanding daily routines.

At the end of the week following the celebration of hearts and affection a Citizenship Party was held for the associates in a neighboring borough. Only four associates from the Village of Poe were allowed to attend, Two of a Kind, Bobby Kennedy, Winnie the Pooh and Crown Jewel. The issue of homework completed in the castles was one of the primary disqualifying factors. Neither the life of the Dragons nor the flight of the Drones created a high enough level of expectations nor tight enough ring of accountability to earn the usual suspects an invitation to the Citizenship Party. Indeed by most scales of justice they would weigh in as outlaws worthy of immediate incarceration, if not deportation. Not so surprisingly, as the four good citizens departed, only Marie Antoinette expressed any sorrow about not being included.

To the Groundhog this week seemed like an unusually long one even though it had been shortened by the one day that had been given in memory of the dead presidents. The promise of the Prophet that had been seen in his gesture of the secret lollipop had passed with his continued defiance and efforts to set the stage for Friar Tuck's performances. As the day came to an end he decided to undertake the effort to visit other guardians whose reputations suggested that they had mastered the skills needed to transcend the Dragons and Drones. From them he hoped to find the secrets that could be shared with Master Poe. He recalled a traveler that he had read about in the Great Beyond who wrote "Letters from the Planet Earth." He committed himself to undertaking such a project and preparing a series of "Letters from the Guardians" that would shed light on the life of a teacher in keeping the fires burning in The Land Set Aside for Learning.

A Box of Chocolates

In the Village of Poe the Groundhog and Master Poe gradually came to understand how the metaphor of life being like a box of chocolates, mistakenly left on a delivery truck on a ninety-five degree day in Georgia, could very easily be applied to the world view of the Prophet and the usual suspects. In his complicated young life there were probably many moments of surprise when things almost seemed to go well but mostly there were probably more moments of disappointment when what he was fed fell short of what he was expecting. The assortment of guardians assembled in The Land Set Aside for Learning was analogous to the assortment of candies in a drug store box of chocolates. Rather than accomplishing the intended purpose of providing him with multiple opportunities to develop positive connections and experience the joy of belonging to a supportive community they forced him to stretch his level of trust which was already very low and take risks in believing in those he barely knew.

The Groundhog recalled a time in the not so distant past when young associates were put in the charge of one guardian who had the sole responsibility for their development. The extent of contact between the associate and the guardian during those early developmental years truly empowered the guardians to counterbalance the effects of the dragons and the castles where they abide. For an associate like the Prophet the Groundhog wondered if a more stable relationship would not suit him better than the constant stream of guardians who were sent to help him.

Each day that the Prophet entered the Village he had to make choices, like opening that box of assorted chocolates. Several days each week began with the "group" meeting with Mind Reader and Colonel Hogan and five of the most notorious suspects. Certainly there had to be some almonds in the assortment but maybe the Prophet had been hoping for chocolate covered cherries. From the group meeting he moved to the Village of Poe and the young Master but having experienced the disappointment of the cherries this time he hoped for caramel nugget but got coconut slivers. Soon the Groundhog arrived looking like cashews but only offering toffee. By mid-morning he found his way to the Soup Lady who appeared to be offering some chocolate covered raisins but by now his desire was for peanuts. Then there were the interventions and choices posed by the Man of Music, the Woman of Many Colors, the Market Woman, Princess Leia, Lt. Uhora and the Emperor and the assortment of guardians who challenged him to be nourished by consuming some part of them.

The guardians of The Land Set Aside for Learning did not appear to understand that more guardians intervening did not lead to better intervention. More choices did not lead to better choices. And that quite possibly the Prophet could not see the advantage of this wide assortment and instead with each bite he tried to discover where he could find peace in the space between the chocolate covering of their expectations and the unanticipated filling of their tolerance. The possibility of a restricted diet of M&M's was not an option. After a while he approached everyone with the same suspicion and lack of trust that to take a bite would only lead to disappointment and quickly bring him to the limits of their tolerance. This was what he was raised on in the castle outside the walls of The Land Set Aside for Learning. To protect himself from the distaste he chose to treat all of the chocolates the same and allow none close enough to hurt him, in effect developing an aversion to all chocolates. His secret yearning for chocolate covered cornmeal, which his mother had always prepared in their quiet time, out of sight of the dragon, went undiscovered.

Most of the Prophet's time in the Village was spent escaping opportunities to engage in his learning. The banking system and rating scales that offered some form of delayed gratification were only periodic interruptions of his solitude where he seemed to quietly dance with his demons. From his isolated domicile he watched the world go by and reluctantly went about the business of the day with as little commitment as possible. Every now and then he immersed himself in an activity involving numbers or artwork but for the most part life was like a box of melted chocolates being served to someone with a chocolate allergy. Moses and Friar Tuck seemed to bring him pleasure during their time in the Room for Eating but their antics never offered the potential of leading to any constructive choices. He could join with them or remain in isolation. The Groundhog often spoke to them about the challenge of living like the Three Musketeers and the alternative lifestyle of the Three Stooges but he knew the unity of the trinity was too weak to choose the former. The three of them were living off the land like early adolescent drop-ins, satisfied to scavenge the silver off the Kisses and throw away the chocolate.

In the week following the celebration of the leaders of the Great Beyond the Prophet served two early morning detentions. On the final day of the week he did battle with Colonel Hogan during the group meeting that was intended to help him with his choices. Without the "group" he would have no interaction with Colonel Hogan and now that interaction led to a two day suspension the following week. Somehow the guardians of The Land Set Aside for Learning expected him to incorporate the meeting and his new chocolate choice into his life as something to look forward to, perhaps like a chocoholic approaches an abstinence meeting.

Life was truly difficult for the Prophet and as the Groundhog watched he prayed that somewhere in the assortment of guardians in The Land Set Aside for Learning the Prophet would find some peace that he could believe in, some moment during the day when he really wanted to be there and was engaged in the life that was passing him by. He prayed that he could find that piece of chocolate that the Prophet would consume and look forward to having more each day and in that way make the Village of Poe his refuge in the same way that he found solace around his mother. He realized that when an associate was raised on and sustained by chocolate covered cornmeal it takes time and trust to develop a taste for any other kind. Time and trust were just two of the many things that the Prophet did not have in abundance.

And on the Third Day

On the day following the Prophet's two-day suspension the Groundhog arrived at the Village of Poe anticipating seeing the young associate at the south end in his state of isolation. However, upon entering the village Master Poe summoned him and shared that the Prophet would not be in the village that day. He explained that the Prophet had been brought to The Land Set Aside for Learning by his mother earlier that morning. When she reported to the main gate she indicated that he had been anticipating his return and was unruly in the castle and that even though his parents were able to transport him to The Land Set Aside for Learning his disposition suggested that admitting him would only lead to another suspension. Master Poe was asked to send his work for the day to the main gate and he was taken back to the castle.

As the Groundhog listened to the series of events, he imagined the scene in the castle that morning as the oatmeal was being served and the Prophet found the courage to tell the dragon that he had had enough and was not going to The Land Set Aside for Learning. He imagined the father and the mother taking turns explaining the importance of his attendance. He imagined the final decree from the father telling him to be strong and "do what you gotta do." He saw the Prophet being drug out to the transportation vehicle along with his siblings protesting the sentence to continued solitude in the village and the silence of the ride interspersed with proclamations of "liberty or death." Upon their arrival he envisioned the Prophet sitting outside the gates in the transportation vehicle, his coat transformed into a straight jacket with his backpack twisted into shackles on his ankles, staring ahead with the tracks of tears on his cheeks. From that vantage point, he watched the other associates joyfully coming through the gates, not noticing him in the silence of his pain. He believed in his mother and in the end she came through and delivered him back to the castle.

Off and on throughout the day the Groundhog wondered what had taken the Prophet so long to get to this point of refusing to come to the place of his misery. His refusal would be the logical response of any healthy guardian. Who would willingly stay in a place where they felt isolated and miserable? None of the interventions had focused on how he felt or why he felt the way he did. Perhaps the Prophet was on to something that the guardians had not seen. Maybe for him life in the castle offered a different sense of belonging and security and therefore could be more productive than life in the village. The Groundhog thought about how little he really knew about the castle where the Prophet resided. Certainly he had less than positive impressions about the father and older sibling but in reality these were only snapshots perhaps not of them at their finer moments. Perhaps they could respond to the Prophet's needs in ways that the guardians were not equipped. The mother certainly offered more hope than any and being sequestered in the castle would certainly lead to more time with her.

The Groundhog visited the GodE.S., soliciting her assessment of the assortment of chocolates and the subsequent events. She indicated that she had no role in the "group" or preparation of the personnel involved in the various plans. She also expressed her concern that the decision to concede to the wishes of the Prophet to not attend The Land Set Aside for Learning might be the beginning of a journey in the wrong direction, down the proverbial slippery slope, because it indirectly gives him the sense of power to make the choice whenever he saw fit. These choices were the purview of the adults and rarely afforded to young associates who lack the wisdom to make such far reaching decisions.

Later in the day the Groundhog encountered the Soup Lady and recognized how light on her feet she had seemed of late. She greeted him in passing and took a moment to explain how pleased she was with the progress being made by her group during the Unhappy Hour, progress which coincidentally had been chartered in the absence of the Prophet. She was quite aware of these concurrent events and shared that she was working on a plan to offer a private unhappy hour each day to the Prophet. This possibility intrigued the Groundhog who quietly wondered if the Soup Lady really believed that being beaten up alone felt any better than a public whipping. It was clear that the Prophet's absence had far reaching implications, even for the associates who were returning from the Unhappy Hour each day with handfuls of money from the Soup Lady.

As the sun set, the Groundhog sat on his perch at the south end of the village thinking about the domicile that had stood vacant for three days. From this vantage point his glance happened to turn to Moses who was positioning himself in line behind Crown Jewel. His interest in Crown Jewel had continued to grow since the day of the Four Corners. She seemed to be pleasantly concerned about his proximity to her in the line and he seemed overly concerned about the Groundhog's gaze. In his usual opulent manner, Moses gave the Groundhog a gesture that could be read "Why are you watching me?" or "Let me steal the jewels!" He whispered to Crown Jewel who then turned to look at the Groundhog with a look of embarrassment, as she tried to develop some distance between the two of them. The Groundhog continued his gaze thinking that in the absence of the Prophet, Moses' attention was now turning to other areas of interest. The Groundhog slowly went to Master Poe with a precautionary note to be sure to separate Moses and Crown Jewel in all future promenades. He had not realized the blessing that the Prophet had been.

In making his way through the streets of The Land Set Aside for Learning at the end of the day, he thought about the light of the Prophet. He wondered if anyone had seen that light and entertained the thought of "home schooling" rather than I.E.P.s or smaller classrooms or Emotional Support. Could the answer be as simple as his need to be in the security of his castle? Could his father and mother and the Emperor be engaged in some mutually respectful conversation of an alternative plan? He wondered about his role and if he would be acceptable to the Prophet. He thought about the rope he had prayed for while watching the Boys on a Raft. He remembered the scripture "And I heard the voice of the Lord saying "Who will go for us? Who shall I send? And I replied, saying "Here, Here am I. Send Me." On the third day the Prophet had rolled the stone away and his light was a sign for those to look beyond his faults and see his needs. On the fourth day, the snows returned and the series of snow days, morning detentions, suspensions and more snow days continued but now there was a light for all to see.

Letters from the Guardians #1

As the Groundhog journeyed through The Land Set Aside for Learning he sought out the advice of the guardians who had toiled there for many years, as well as those who labored in the Great Beyond, believing that in their collective wisdom answers to the challenges posed by the associates in the Village of Poe could be found. He asked several of them to share the most important lessons that they had learned about teaching. He promised only to identify them by the place that they had attended in preparing to become a teacher.

The contents of the following letter came from a guardian trained in Happy Valley:

"Thank you for the opportunity to share these brief reflections on lessons learned in a lifetime of teaching and learning. I pray that they prove to be of some assistance and/or comfort to those who touch the future.

The most important lesson for being an effective teacher is one of those that you were taught in kindergarten, LOOK. The sky, the mountains, the rivers, the streets, the alleys, the houses, the flowers, the broken bottles, the broken people, the birds, the dogs, the snow and the rain, the young, the old, the whole world, all of it is your curriculum. It is constantly changing so never stop looking and being amazed. The day that you stop looking, stop teaching.

SHARE because what you have others need and what you need others will have.

LUNCH whenever possible should be eaten with your students. You will learn much about them. Dinner whenever possible should be eaten with your family. They also need you. If you can't keep this straight you are spending too much time in school, so go home for dinner.

BELIEVE the possibilities are endless even when the odds seem insurmountable. Success comes in so many small ways that you may not see at any given moment but each moment that you are there you and your students are learning something.

The ALAMO is not your room. So fight the impulse to close the door in order to save your students. The cavalry does come. Help is all around you. When you close your doors you limit the possibilities for the success of your students and yourself. There is always another new day.

SUMMER is the time to rest and to learn. Although you may never tire of being a teacher you do need the time to rest as you learn. Plan your summer wisely. It passes too quickly.

HOLD HANDS when you can regardless of the age of your students. In a time when "touching" is under such scrutiny nothing says you care like holding someone's hand. It's a lost art.

SCRULES are the endless list of school rules that adorn too many buildings and classrooms. Keep your list small and be sure to include the Golden Rule.

LISTEN to the sounds around you, the horns blowing, the jack hammers, the continuous announcements, the clamor in the hall, the light fixtures, the heating system, the laughter, the cafeteria, the office chatter, the high heels, the squeaking shoes, the pencil sharpeners, the little and the big arguments, and best of all the silence at the beginning and end of the day. Your eyes and ears are your portals to the world. Keep them open and enjoy the recordings.

KEYS provide access. Reading, writing and arithmetic have always been the keys to accessing the future. In all that you do remember that our profession is the key to their future so develop it as if your life depended on it.

STOP to reflect every now and then on the things that made you want to become a teacher and the things that you hoped you would do when you became the teacher that you hoped to be. Stop doing the things that you said you would never do. Stop putting off doing those things that you remember good teachers doing. Stop holding on to those things that keep you from being the best teacher that you can be.

The Groundhog thought the correspondence to be the most motivational and so he decided to share it in the first of the letters from those prepared at Happy Valley. Two other guardians from Mount Nittany submitted their letters for consideration with each offering somewhat more succinct lessons.

"95+% of students will behave the way you allow them to behave and perform academically to the level you expect of them. If your students are not behaving the way you want, or achieving the way you want, look to yourself as both the problem and the solution."

"Good relationships with your students not only make teaching more satisfying, but help achieve more in your classroom."

"Teaching is/should be equal parts reflection and implementation. To reflect on one's practice is to grow and improve. To question one's efficacy is to be aware of the progress or lack of progress being made by one's students."

While the Groundhog pondered the thinking of those prepared in the largest teacher preparation colony, he looked forward to hearing the thoughts of others. He hoped that he would be able to share the wisdom of the veteran guardians with Master Poe and in some way contribute to a more reflective community of guardians throughout The Land Set Aside for Learning. He saw the extent of the lessons in the letters from the two guardians who had been prepared in the place known for its slippery rocks and anxiously anticipated digesting their content.

A League of Her Own

When the Prophet returned from his suspension he was accompanied by his father. Two days after his return the Groundhog happened to run into the father standing at the entry and decided to engage him in a conversation about the Prophet's progress. The father explained that he had come to The Land Set Aside for Learning after taking his son for a psychological evaluation at a local mental health facility. However, his trip had been unsuccessful because of a mix-up in the timing of the testing.

As they talked, the father inquired as to whether the Groundhog had heard that he had met with Colonel Hogan about putting his hands on the Prophet. (Apparently this was the incident that led to the suspension the week before.) He explained that he wanted "them" to know that no one was allowed to "put their hands on him" and that what they were really trying to do was keep associates from his old neighborhood out of The Land Set Aside for Learning. The Groundhog marveled at his odd sense of justice and his self-perception as the sole caretaker of the Prophet. There was definitely no "in loco parentis" in his view of the world.

The conversation between the two lasted for about five minutes when Jada Pinkett wandered by and stopped to get the Groundhog's attention on her way from the Medicine Woman back to the Village of Poe. She slowly approached the Groundhog and with her head tilted slightly to the side, as if trying to measure his height from a different perspective, she waved and said "Hello." Since she was less than five feet from him the wave seemed a little unnecessary and most reflective of her innocence. Her greeting clearly was meant as an interruption and command to talk to me. Taking note of her demand the father of the Prophet ended his discourse and quickly departed.

Jada and the Groundhog proceeded to the Village of Poe at a very leisurely pace, which was Jada's way. She was never in a hurry to get anywhere or say anything. Her disposition always suggested that there was more to read between the lines of her words and movements than could be found in the literal translations. She definitely approached life in her own quiet way. The Groundhog had grown very fond of her during his journey in part because she was a loner like him and her quiet nature was easy to be around as well as a challenge to figure out.

In recent weeks Jada had taken over being last in line. Whereas the male associates would push and force themselves against the wall at the end of the village to ensure being last, Jada would simply not get in line. When the other associates lined up to leave the village Jada would move towards the end of the line. If any of the usual suspects positioned themselves to be last, she would have no part in their shenanigans. Instead, she would begin walking around the village looking at the ground like a little league right fielder who got bored with the game and began searching the grass for a four leaf clover. She'd patiently wait until the line had left the village. Not only was she determined to be last but her determination was so strong that she didn't mind being 40 feet behind the line.

The Groundhog asked Jada about her desire to be last in line. Like with so many things she said she didn't know why. This one activity was the only assertive act that Jada committed all day. It didn't matter where the associates were headed, whether to eat, play, music, science, art, math or the Unhappy Hour, last to arrive or return was where she had decided she wanted to be. Needless to say, at times it appeared that she was wandering the streets of The Land Set Aside for Learning alone since she was so far behind. This pattern of behavior didn't seem to bother the guardians as much as one might think. Jada was sweet and quiet and so tiny that she moved almost like a cat and everyone knows there is no return on telling a cat to walk faster.

In the Room for Eating Jada had only three associates that she spent any time eating with, June O'Sullivan, Amelia Badilia and Two of a Kind. June and Amelia were actually attached at the hip and Two was a "wanna be" with Winnie the Pooh and Crown Jewel. As often as not Jada could be found sitting alone not eating the food she had gotten off the menu. The Groundhog had taken note that only June O'Sullivan had poorer eating habits than Jada. June brought lunches to school that centered around a soft pretzel and other starches. Jada on the other hand accessed the school lunch menu but chose not to eat most of the things that were served. The fact that the other associates asked why she put the food on her platter but didn't eat it did not bother her in the least. She simply did not respond. The one entrée that she consumed as if it were the last supper was macaroni salad, which was on no one's top ten list.

Each day in the village the Groundhog made a point to visit with Jada at her domicile. He'd always offer his assistance and she would politely decline. To say that her writing skills were less than proficient would be like saying chicken coops have an interesting odor. Jada rarely completed her assignments and turned in her homework about as often as the seasons changed. Master Poe confided that her response to whether she did her homework was a simple "no." The Groundhog pressed her about their evolving relationship in which she had begun to eat with him everyday and how it made him feel when she would not allow him to help her. Her facial expression reminded him of his grandmother when she would look at him after he uttered something that had been poorly thought out. Like being last in line, Jada seemed determined to not do her work her own way.

Because Jada was a loner she sought out the company of the Groundhog in the Room for Eating when Master Poe determined that Crown Jewel and Winnie the Pooh needed a little space from the usual suspects. The Groundhog's location became the dividing line between the males and the females during the time for eating. When the most popular females moved to the south end, that had been the exclusive domain of Jada, she headed to the middle next to the Groundhog, preferring his questions over the never ending drama of her new neighbors. Seated with the Groundhog and Marie Antoinette, who happened to be the best eater of all the associates, Jada seemed to talk more than at any other time of day and displayed quite a sense of humor. Marie had a younger sister and her confidence and maturity allowed Jada to be herself without the competition of the exchanges with the other female associates.

Jada was truly an enigma to the Groundhog. It was hard for anyone not to like her because she posed no threat, was never oppositional and always at least pretended to do what she was told. When told to go to her domicile and complete an assignment, she'd go and sit and do the minimal. Grades didn't matter to her. She was the lone female of the six that attended the Unhappy Hour. Where that might have bothered some, Jada could not have cared less. She put in her time and did as little as possible. When told to read independently, Jada would take out a book and lie on the floor and appear to be reading. She was quiet almost to the point of invisibility. The idea that she might not be reading was a reoccurring one.

The Groundhog often wondered if she actually possessed any of the skills that she was feigning indifference. Because she came from a family that spoke two languages he asked the Guardian of ESL to speak with her. Nothing in Jada's conversations in the Room for Eating suggested any difficulty with the language. She had shared that her father and grandparents spoke another language at home. She and her mother knew the language but didn't speak it. She seemed to delight in listening to the Rock and A-Rod speak the language but would never converse with them. She'd only share with the Groundhog that she knew what they were talking about. Oddly enough, Jada was interested in the print media and on occasion would bring a book she was reading over to the Groundhog to share a point of interest. One book that she found particularly interesting was a language book that taught basic conversations in English, French, Spanish and German. Her questions indicated that she clearly could read.

Having Jada around was one of those positive challenges that helped balance the Groundhog's day and offset the antics of the usual suspects. Her laughter and sporadic chatter in the Room for Eating made going there a delight even though almost ten minutes could be lost on the trip there because of her commitment to being last. When walking with her the Groundhog never knew whether she would prefer to be behind, in front or beside him. Visiting her under her domicile while she was reading was always an adventure in reading her exasperated facial expressions. Jada was forever doing it her way, playing in a league of her own, and the Groundhog was determined to find a way into her game and learn the rules so that her skills could be transferred into the game of life in the Great Beyond. He feared that without intervention she would remain beneath the radar and the light that she possessed would continue to flicker in the shadows of her quiet demeanor.

Letters from the Guardians #2

The Groundhog received letters from two guardians who were prepared in the place known as Slippery Rock. Together they had been in the teaching profession for over half a century. The Groundhog sat at the feet of each of them as they quite coincidentally shared ten of the most important lessons that they had learned on the road to becoming successful guardians.

The guardian from the town across the road from the Village of Poe wrote –

"My 10 most important lessons are:

To create community, each of us needs all of us, and all of us need each of us. Building Community in the classroom is one of the most important things that help bond a class of students together for the duration of a school year.

Procedures help the classroom run like a well-oiled machine. Procedures are different than rules, and help students to know how to do everyday things so that the class of many people runs smoothly. The way you do things should make every student feel like part of the community.

Keep rules few and simple. I have three, Be Safe, Be Kind, Do Your Job!

Be Prepared. Well-planned lessons are not created in 5 minutes. It is better to be over-planned, than under-planned.

Keep a Poem in your Pocket. A daily 5-10 minute dose of poetry can improve students' fluency; develop knowledge of figurative language, rhyming, rhythm, and description and help prepare for high-stakes testing. But perhaps most importantly, it speaks to the soul.

Send in the Clowns! Everyone loves a good laugh. Students enjoy a lighthearted approach to their lessons. Humor can defuse tense situations. Have a bag of tricks. Don't be afraid to be corny or silly. Students love it and work harder for you.

Always make time to Read Aloud! Among the benefits reading aloud provides are: improves vocabulary, builds background knowledge and provides opportunities for the teacher to model reading strategies taught in reading class. Besides, it is great fun.

Growing Readers: Creating a lifelong love of reading. Fill your room with as many books as you can and arrange them in a child friendly way. Give students time to read their independent books and let them have choices in what they read.

We're in the 21st Century! An informative, up-to-date webpage does wonders to impress parents and students. By maintaining it daily, it shows your commitment to the students and that goes a long way with parents.

I Touch the Future…I Teach! Sometimes you will get discouraged. Teaching is an all-consuming endeavor. Sometimes you will be underappreciated and criticized. But, don't despair; all it takes is one hug from a student or special note from a parent to erase all of those negative moments."

After sitting with the most senior guardian, the Groundhog travelled to the second guardian who had been prepared at the place known for its slippery rocks. She was known as the GodE.S. and the Room with No Chairs was under her dominion. The GodE.S. wrote –
"If you are not willing to follow through, don't say it out loud.
    If you don't respect the students or find something good in them, they won't respect you.
    You must be willing to act like a fool at times to have the students understand the lesson being taught.
    When dealing with challenging students don't do the expected.
    A student throwing a desk will throw it further than you expect.
    Find the time to be with coworkers in a social setting and DON'T talk about the kids.
    Discipline is more important to have than good lesson plans.
    Not all things work with all students.
    What works one week may not work the next.
    Coworkers have so much knowledge; share your skills and ideas."

The Groundhog took the twenty lessons provided by the guardians from the place known for its slippery rocks and began turning them over in his head. He appreciated the time they had taken to compose their ideas as well as their willingness to talk about the associates that had touched them in various ways, the rewards of their work, and how in so many ways their sense of who they are was inextricably tied to being a guardian. Because of their successes teaching had indeed become a way of life and each year and each class represented a new beginning on the journey of a lifetime. He prayed that their lessons would become a beacon for those who followed.

New World Order

On the third day of the final week of the second month of the year the Groundhog took a holiday and went for a walk along the waterway, a place that he had often sought solace. As he walked he began thinking about how so much had changed since the time he was a young associate. He remembered how chewing gum seemed to be the primary obsession of the guardians of old. According to his recollection the schrule against chewing gum was tantamount to the Eleventh Commandment. Gum chewing was somehow related to almost every aspect of an associates' life, like character, intellect, class, health and even morality. It was as if the guardians of old believed that gum was the determining factor of the associates' life in the Great Beyond as well as the Here After. But now gum had fallen pretty low on the guardians' list of things to obsess over.

Gum had been replaced by line décor. At almost any moment on any day somewhere in The Land Set Aside for Learning a guardian could be heard giving instructions related to getting in line, standing in line, walking in line, talking in line, waiting in line, how to face in line, when the line should start, when the line should stop, where the line should stop, which side the line should proceed on, how to turn corners, how much space should be between each associate, how to keep the line together, who should be where in line- first, last, not next to him, nowhere near her, and on and on ad infinitum. Some of the guardians even attached their happiness to the movement of the lines and would constantly remind the associates that something about the line was "not making me happy" or demanding that they "make me happy."

It wasn't long before the Groundhog came to see that there was no area of instruction so universally embraced and passionately delivered as line décor that was not assessed on the associate's periodic report card. Had it been, it would have undoubtedly been right at the top where "Citizenship" used to be. In fact, lines had become so important that somewhere out there in the Great Beyond the Groundhog sensed that all of the line preparation had to lead to a better more fulfilling way of life for the associates who mastered the requirements.

Along with the devaluing of gum was the disregard for shirttails. In the days of old any male caught with his shirt out of his pants was mercilessly chastised by the guardians and subjected to some form of punishment. No longer was wearing a shirt that was not tucked into your pants considered an act of defiance. In the new world order the clothing of the males were more often than not two sizes too large and the females two sizes to small. On many days it appeared as if the males were wearing their fathers' clothes and the females their little sisters' garments.

What used to be classified as "underwear" was no longer a private matter. The males and females alike seemed to have their under garments on display with the most decorative colors and patterns. The universal white suggesting cleanliness was a thing of the past. Other than the occasional ridicule by the lunatic fringe and usual suspects that accompanied the spotting of a "plumber's crack", no one seemed to care about the formerly very personal hidden garments.

Next on the list of what was but is no more was the preoccupation with shoes and more specifically the tying of shoes. Somewhere buried in the Groundhogs memory was the idea that "play" shoes, and dress shoes and school shoes were more than just a notion for the rich. Play clothes and school clothes also seemed to be distinct. None of this was clear to the Groundhog as he walked. Everyday was now open to whatever attire was worn. Even though it occasionally came up, the guardians had abandoned the battle to ensure that shoes were tied so that associates would not "trip and kill themselves." Perhaps history had suggested this improbability.

Strangely enough, sitting had also changed. Where once keeping ones feet on the floor while seated was a cardinal schrule now associates sat on their legs, on the back of chairs, and with their feet pulled up into the chair. Standing around the desk was also tolerated. For some associates in the Village of Poe just staying in the room was a victory. This mobility of the associates was commensurate with the mobility of their desks which no longer were anchored and seemed to be in constant gradual movement towards the guardian.

The Groundhog stopped to rest on a bench and suddenly recalled how lunch was once a meal eaten at home or with a neighbor in the middle of the day. No one ever went home for lunch anymore. In fact many of the associates now ate breakfast, lunch and an afternoon snack in The Land Set Aside for Learning. The lunch menu now had more items than the Groundhog remembered having at the occasional restaurant that he dined. Even choosing milk meant making a choice between five flavors. Choice seemed to have replaced conformity, consistency and compliance everywhere.

Suddenly the Groundhog's thoughts were jolted back into the moment when he recalled the occasional slap on the back of the head for drifting off in class. Any associate caught day dreaming, or even worse sleeping in class, was subject to a rude awakening. Then there were the omnipresent wooden instruments designed to cripple your hands or "warm the seat of your pants," a notion that seemed terribly euphemistic. The guardians of old always proclaimed that administering those behavior modification techniques hurt them more than it hurt the associates. Somehow, the Groundhog never could figure out why the guardians could not see an easy mutually agreed upon solution to that dilemma.

As he rested, he heard the rumblings of a yellow bus passing and was warmed by the thoughts of walking to school with his childhood friends and all the games they would make up. Buses had taken over now. "Too far" had been redefined as ten minutes from home. Danger was everywhere and "school safeties" had all but disappeared. Associates came to school with bottles of water and bottles of hand sanitizers. The cloak room, once a favorite place to escape to or be placed in solitary isolation had been abolished, just totally wiped out of the buildings. His head began to spin. Slowly he pulled himself up and began the return trip when he remembered that it was not so long ago that he had taken this walk with the father of the Prophet. He thought about how much parents seemed to have changed but the day was so lovely he decided to hold those thoughts for another walk, perhaps on a rainy day.

Bad Doctors

One Saturday morning the Groundhog was awakened by a call. The caller indicated that a messenger from Up South in the Great Beyond was in town to spread the news about reforming the guardians and ensuring the learning of the associates. Since these issues were near to the Groundhog's heart he immediately embarked on the journey to hear the good news. He did not have to travel far because the forum was being held in the neighboring province, a place notorious for outspoken prognosticators and institutions immersed in calamitous operations.

The meeting began shortly after his arrival. A panel of ten of the Most High was introduced along with the newly elected mayor and soon to be deported chief of learning. Each of them gave welcoming remarks of no substance and expressed their appreciation for the work that had been done by the keynote prognosticator from Up South. They were immediately seated apart from each other on the first row and then the word was spoken. The prognosticator quickly whipped the audience into frenzy as he spoke about the "bad" guardians and the need to close the Land Set Aside for Learning in order to get rid of them. The members of the panel nodded their approval and shouted words of encouragement and approval. The larger audience stood and applauded as he warned about the "scourge" of the education profession and wasted financial resources. Following his comments a lawmaker with designs on running for governor shared his words of folly.

The Groundhog sat quiet and listened in amazement. When the meeting ended and he began his journey home he decided to write the legislator. That night he penned the following letter:

"Dear Senator;

I was in attendance at the meeting on Saturday, March 13, 2010, for the MLKLDI's "Blueprint for Prosperity Forum III: Equity in Education." To say that I found the comments from the keynote Prognosticator, offensive would be a gross understatement. I found the primary gist of his comments to be down right insulting in both delivery and content.

As I listened to him talking about "bad guardians" I wondered what Dr. King would have thought about his continued use of the phrase "I swear to God." Would that be a phrase acceptable to our children, teachers or legislators? Could his inflammatory comments about "bad teachers," that there can be no good teaching if bad teaching is going on in the building" be heard has anything short of an indictment of all teachers? Could it be applied to police, lawyers, doctors and God forbid state legislators? Would his solution, "You have to begin by closing some of the schools." also apply? Would you suggest that we start by closing some police stations, hospitals, health care facilities, prisons and state capitols to get rid of the "bad" people who work there?

I watched the panel of distinguished guests sit there nodding their approval of his guardian and union bashing and I wondered why people who spent most of their lives in the field of education would tacitly support his denunciation of guardians. The silly expressions on their faces and the empty unresponsive comments that followed made me think of Dr. King's words that "History will remember us not because of the deeds of a few wicked men but because of the silence of so many who stood by and did nothing." There were superintendents from several provinces in attendance and the one question that I wanted to ask of them was how many "bad guardians" had they tried to fire in their entire careers. What would be your guess? Rather than engaging in the "honest" dialogue and open forum that they pretended to be having, they sat there applauding and offering "Amens" and "hallelujahs."

I had hoped that when you took the stage as a member of the Senate Education Committee and gubernatorial candidate you might sound a voice of reason but instead you took the low road and joined the sheep that were howling like wolves. You mentioned that your mother was a guardian but you didn't mention how she would have felt if she were sitting there in the auditorium. Was she one of those guardians that didn't go to the class next door and do something to that bad guardian? Are you one of those legislators that won't expose the bad legislators to the public? Was your mother one of those bad teachers who didn't want her own son to go to the schools that she taught in? How many schools in your district will you recommend closing? You stood there praising the Big Prognosticator for all of his sacrifices but what about his message to the community. What about his message in our "Blueprint for Prosperity?" What did he leave us with that caused you to jump on his bandwagon? What did you leave us with?

You shared the analogy of being on a hospital gurney and the doctor acknowledging that he couldn't help you. Would you suggest firing all of the doctors that have been warning you all of your life about the eventual consequences of your eating, lack of exercise and family history on your health or do you accept your responsibility for your present condition. In many ways guardians are like doctors and students are like patients, families, food and physical and mental exercise have a lot to do with the outcome of their work.

I hope that you simply missed the opportunity to engage in an honest dialogue and that you really don't believe that closing schools is the solution and bad guardians are the problem. But if you do believe the message that the Big Prognosticator delivered then I hope you spread the word as you travel seeking support for your bid for Governor of the Commonwealth. Honesty in government is something that all politicians proclaim, even the bad ones. Please put them on notice that you will be exposing them along with the "bad guardians" bill as part of your platform. You know that you have the support of people like the clamoring multitude that was in attendance.

Be the Change!"

Once the letter was done the Groundhog offered a silent prayer mentioning Jada Pinkett, Moses, the Prophet, Jeremiah, Friar Tuck, Mo Betta, Master Poe, the Soup Lady, the GodE.S. and all of the associates and guardians in The Land Set Aside for Learning.

Maybe Tomorrow

One Thursday morning Master Poe requested that Jada Pinkett sit with the Groundhog and complete an exercise that had been assigned to the associates earlier in the week. It was apparent that he was concerned about her continued pattern of not completing any of her assignments. Upon hearing his instructions Jada slowly proceeded to the south end of the village where the Groundhog was perched. As she approached him she made a right turn and rather than pulling into his quarters she went about six posts over, slightly out of earshot. There she stood in a hovering mode, doing nothing in particular, seeming to be counting the pebbles on the ground.

The Groundhog, recognizing this behavior pattern as one of those that led to the passage of time and the accomplishment of very little, called out to her in a loud whisper. Jada turned, acknowledging receipt of the message, smiled and continued life in the slow and easy mode. Again the Groundhog called out requesting Jada to come over and sit with him. She repeated her response of smiling without moving.

From his perch the Groundhog continued to watch Jada for almost five minutes. Her passive standoff was finally interrupted by Master Poe calling out and ordering her to sit down and get to work. At that point she came over and stood before him as if awaiting sentencing. The Groundhog explained the assignment of finding five words with the prefix "un" and five with the suffix "ful." Jada looked up into his eyes, smiled and whispered "I didn't hear anything you said." Slowly she took a seat beside him continuing her unwillingness to participate. Jada was sweet that way, never one to fight the tide but always willing to float along without offering any open resistance or putting in any effort to the task at hand.

Soon the allotted time ended and Jada returned to her domicile without making any progress on the assignment. It was time to eat and the unrelenting march of time meant that the language arts battle could be postponed for another day. As the associates made their way to the Room for Eating, Jada and the Groundhog walked together far behind the procession. While they were walking the Groundhog asked her about her unwillingness to work with him on her assignment. He shared that his feelings were hurt by her sharing her mid-day meal everyday but not cooperating with him on the primary reason for being in the village. Her response to his inquiry was a simple "I don't know." He smiled back at her and thought "So much for leveraging the relationship into productivity."

The following day Jada was instructed to pay another visit to the Groundhog to work on a "packet" about Harriett Tubman. Jada's assignment required her to read a short story, make a KWL outline, and write a poem about the character. The Groundhog was somewhat familiar with the character because the Prophet had held up a picture of her, proclaiming that she looked like the Groundhog's sister when he greeted him that morning. He confirmed the Prophet's assessment by assuring him that it actually looked more like his mother than his sister but the two did favor each other. He then thanked the Prophet for recognizing their beauty.

Jada made her way back to the Groundhog's perch, this time positioning herself directly in front of him. Having grown to understand some of the mysteries of Jada from their daily walks to the Room for Eating and sharing their mealtime together, the Groundhog sensed that her reluctance to become engaged in her work with him might stem from her desire to remain invisible which of course was compromised by his presence. He offered her the opportunity to leave the village and meet with him beyond the village gates. After several promptings she agreed that it would be better if they met in seclusion and they quietly exited the village under the gaze of the Prophet and Friar Tuck, two characters that he wished would become less visible.

Soon they found a place to squat at an intersection known as Krot's Corner, not the most private place in The Land Set Aside for Learning, but there they began the work on the Tubman packet. Jada read the story silently and the Groundhog watched her eyes for clues that she might be pretending. As she turned the pages she would occasionally look up and ask for clarification of words e.g., "What's an iron weight?" and "Is this word Moses?" The Groundhog was pleased to see that she was actually comprehending the written word as well as staying on task.

When she was done reading they went over the instructions for writing the outline. The graphic organizer that she had to complete had four sections without lines for the associates to write on. Jada scribbled a few one word answers regarding what she knew about the character. She then looked up at the Groundhog and stated that what she wanted to know about the story was "Nothing" which she began writing in bold letters. As she wrote she said that she thought the word had two "t" and insisted that it did. Neither of her letter "t" was recognizable.

The Groundhog became increasingly concerned about her spelling and penmanship. It occurred to him that her inability to print the words might contribute greatly to her unwillingness to complete and hand in any assignments. Suddenly their work was interrupted by the arrival of a messenger sent by Master Poe summoning Jada back to the village. They agreed to pick up where they left off the same time the next day. For Jada "agreement" simply meant a quiet response of "maybe tomorrow."

Unfortunately tomorrow was not the day following their time at Krot's Corner. When the sun made its trek the following day Jada had returned to her illusive state of non-compliance. She was required to stay inside and work for the 30-minute playtime. For her that was no punishment since she more often than not wandered around by herself when outside. However, on this day work was not on her agenda and during her confinement the Groundhog sat by her domicile and watched her quietly walk around the Village of Poe as if either he or she was invisible. It was as if she believed that the silence of her voice, the absence of writing her assignments, her distance at the end of the line and her unresponsiveness somehow made her invisible and thereby unaccountable.

Habits

With each passing day as he travelled through the streets of The Land Set Aside for Learning the Groundhog became more and more aware of the habitual nature of the inhabitants. Both associates and guardians alike demonstrated consistent patterns of behavior, seemingly unconscious of the impact. As he grew in his understanding he began to see how making a difference in the lives of many of the usual suspects could only be accomplished by interrupting the habits that they had internalized.

Upon entering the village everyday the Groundhog made a point to acknowledge the Prophet, who lived just inside the gate, with the French greeting "Bonjour Monsieur." Each day the Prophet responded with a statement of defiance or rebellion. On some days he would ask "Why are you looking at me?" or "You got something on your chest?" or "You got eye problems?" There was no let up. It was as if he had been programmed to respond to the social greeting with an insult. No matter the greeting, he habitually responded with some form of offensive language.

Friar Tuck had many habits that inhibited him from getting out of his won way, so to speak. Each afternoon when it was time for 20 minutes of silent reading he would sit up and survey the village, as if looking for his parents in a crowded church. Then he would sink down into his seat in a manner that resembled a turtle withdrawing into its shell. After a few minutes he'd get up and start ambling towards the rear of the village. Master Poe would ask why he was moving about. He always gave the same response, "to get a book." This retort was followed by "Why?" One of two reasons was habitually offered something about his mother or else he forgot. This usually took up 15 of the 20 minutes. Finally Tuck would get a book and return to his domicile in time for the transition to the next activity. At that point he'd ask "Can I go to the bathroom?"

In recent weeks four associates in the Village of Poe, Bobby Kennedy, Two of a Kind, Crown Jewel and Winnie the Pooh, had received Homework Honor Roll recognition for completing all of their homework assignments. A bulletin board depicting all of the localities in The Land Set Aside for Learning was periodically updated by Lt. Uhora to provide recognition to those who demonstrated the habit of doing their homework. Some localities had as many as 20 of 24 associates recognized but the Village of Poe was ranked last with only four. The habit of not doing homework had become a way of life for many in the village and this habit seemed engrained into Jada Pinkett's life cycle. When asked about her homework Jada habitually responded with "No" she didn't do it and "I don't know why." That pretty much ended the habitual conversation.

Jada's habit of non-participation was among the most interesting displayed by the usual suspects in the village. On most days she sat quietly fidgeting with things in her desk or rubbing her nose. On a good day getting three or four words on a paper was the extent of the work that could be pulled out of her before she decided it was enough. Any assignment that was not graded, like journaling, homework or group projects, was treated as optional and the habit of not doing it more often than not prevailed. In an attempt to break these habits the Groundhog requested Jada and her closest confidante, Marie Antoinette, come up with an accountability plan. The two enthusiastically embraced the challenge and suggested an assignment checklist that when completed would reward Jada with chocolate candy on a weekly basis.

Each day during the following week Jada reported her progress to the Groundhog. While in the village she slowly began to sit with him and discuss her work. Her disconnect with the other associates served her well as she shut out their peer control of her movements to be near him. He hoped that her proximity would become a habit and facilitate more intimate one on one instructional opportunities.

Justus

One day the Groundhog discovered that there was an unwritten schrule limiting three associates to each side of the table in the Room for Eating. This schrule was most likely established to ensure adequate eating space as well as to minimize overcrowding and the resulting conflict that associates inevitably engaged in when supervision is at a minimum. One consequence of this schrule is that those arriving first get their choice of seating. Another related, but less widely accepted, schrule is that there is no "saving" seats. So, those arriving last have to fend for themselves and if they are law abiding will be eating on the periphery.

One Wednesday afternoon, as Marie Antoinette, Jada and the Groundhog were enjoying the noon repass, their time together was interrupted by the grumblings of Friar Tuck. Tuck was without a desirable seat because the room had been blessed with a surprise visit from the mother of the Prophet. Because Tuck was at the bottom of the totem pole of the usual suspects his customary seat was given to the mother, leaving him in need of a Plan B.

For Tuck any seat not under the spell of his spiritual leader, the Prophet, would be like a date with a painless dentist. Rather than accept an available seat Friar decided to argue for a seat momentarily vacated by Mo Betta. Soon the argument rose to a level that could no longer be ignored. When the Groundhog addressed Friar Tuck he immediately began the customary warrior's chant "How come you…? Why can't I…?" and related whine chants. As he chanted Mo Betta spotted the Emperor and immediately embarked to enlist his aid.

The Emperor, who was stationed nearby, stopped momentarily to hear Mo Betta's plea but his attention was interrupted by a cell phone call. When the call was completed he noticed the Groundhog motioning him to come over to where Mo Betta, Friar Tuck and I'm New were gathered. He approached the group and sensing the dissension took charge by stating that he was not going to be a part of the argument and wanted them to settle it themselves. I'm New, not being one to question authority, immediately got up and gave Mo Betta his seat. The Emperor thanked him and admonished Mo Betta, who was looking violated and confused, to try to talk things out rather than seek the involvement of adults in the future.

Friar Tuck having secured the victory by getting the seat with the unwitting help of the Emperor turned and taunted the Groundhog and Mo Betta. Not wanting to undermine the authority of the Emperor by continuing the discussion the Groundhog reached for a moral to make the episode make sense. He explained to the three associates that sometimes "justice" which means the fair treatment of everyone has to be defined as "just-us," which means we are alone to do good for each other. He went on to say that bullies don't always get what they deserve but those who do good are rewarded because their deeds are the reward that bullies never get. And so, he thanked I'm New for giving up his seat in order to make things better for Mo Betta. He thanked Mo Betta for being able to let the argument go. And, he warned Friar Tuck that the bad deeds that he thought he was getting away with would one day catch up with him.

The Groundhog left the Room for Eating wondering how to make the Emperor aware that having the weak make peace with the bullies does not ensure that justice has been served. This day reinforced his understanding that those who administer justice cannot be blind and must always be mindful that without justice there can me no lasting peace. Simply ending an argument may bring silence between the combatants but beneath the silence Mo Betta's feelings were simmering and might one day surface in a less than productive manner.

The following day the Groundhog spoke with Master Poe about Friar Tuck. When they entered the Room for Eating Tuck was instructed to sit in the less than favorable area near the Groundhog. As usual, Tuck chanted and welled up with tears about the injustice. When he finally sat down he looked at the Groundhog and asked why he was always getting him into trouble. The Groundhog smiled and shared that sitting in the midst of just us is simply Master Poe's way of administering justice. Needless to say this made no sense to Friar who suffered through the meal with unceasing warrior chants.

Profiles in Courage

Spring had come and with it came a sense of urgency for the Groundhog. The mystery of Jada's lack of performance was troubling. After discussing her inability to write with no fewer than five of the guardians, all having varying levels of awareness of her deficiencies, he decided to arrange a meeting with the Emperor.

While sitting at the feet of the Emperor the Groundhog shared his concern that Jada's words on paper were almost illegible. Everything from the formation of her letters, the spatial orientation between the letters and the words, and even the size of the letters were more reflective of a first year associate than one who had spent the better part of four years in the formal pursuit of knowledge. This in and of itself was disheartening but even more troubling was the fact that so many of the guardians were aware but not taking responsibility for addressing her inadequate skills. It was as if Jada had convinced everyone that she was invisible and therefore should be accepted as a non-contributing member of society.

The Emperor listened attentively and reviewed the work sample provided by the Groundhog. He then explained the demands on Master Poe and how they may lead to the acceptance of anything as better than nothing. He spoke of the possible lack of parental support. He asked about the insights of the guardians who were acquainted with her.

Soon the Groundhog grew impatient with the responses. It did not sound like the siren he had hoped to hear was going off. As his heart grew heavy he shared that Jada had one thing that no one else in The Land Set Aside for Learning had. She had him. If time and resources were the obstacle to her success, she had him. If support from the home was the problem, she had him and he'd be willing to visit her in the evenings and give her time on the weekends. He spoke as her parent when saying someone from The Land Set Aside for Learning should be able to state why Jada wrote so poorly and what was being done to correct it. He reaffirmed that she had him with all the passion he could muster.

The Emperor suggested that the Groundhog's concerns about Jada should first be addressed within the walls of The Land Set Aside for Learning prior to developing any intervention strategies between the Groundhog and Jada's parents. The Groundhog shared that he would be away for a week and upon his return he intended to make Jada his "raison d'etre." The Emperor agreed to continue the conversation with the appropriate guardians.

Before taking his holiday the Groundhog met with Jada and Marie Antoinette and discussed a plan for getting Jada to complete her assignments. The two of them suggested a weekly checklist of assignments with a four star rating scale. If more than half of the assignments were completed with at least two stars Jada would receive one bite-sized candy bar for each completed assignment. They agreed to develop the checklist during his absence. The Groundhog left with the sense that between the Emperor and Jada's commitment things would soon turn around.

A week later the Groundhog returned to the Village with a renewed sense of purpose. When he entered he was informed that the Emperor and Princess Leia had paid an hour long visit during which time they simply observed the associates. He hoped that Jada was the focus of their time. Early in the day he met with Jada and Marie Antoinette and inquired about the proposed checklist. They apologized for not developing it but did not seem particularly troubled by the neglected responsibility.

He was not to be deterred by this apparent oversight. He requested a list of assignments from Master Poe and created a checklist in a notebook provided by the Master. He reviewed the list with Jada. Each day they met and assessed her progress. More often than not Jada would earn one or two stars, which was reflective of minimal performance. (One star was given for handing it in and two stars for completing the assignment.)

Jada's writing had begun to improve from the use of primary level writing paper. The Groundhog requested the assistance of Madame Katrina who sent Lady Ashford of O.T., who was renowned for her handwriting instruction. Lady Ashford paid an unofficial visit to the village while Jada and the Groundhog were working together. He quickly summarized their efforts. Lady Ashford assessed Jada's skills and went off to secure some "magic paper."

In a short while she returned with sheets of paper with spaces that resembled a scanable application. Each letter had to be printed in a three sided box. She worked with Jada on transcribing her work onto the magic paper. Jada embraced the opportunity to work with Lady Ashford. She filled the entire page and insisted on continuing into her time for eating. True to her nature she refused to stop writing until after the Groundhog had left her to go to the Room for Eating.

The Groundhog was excited about the breakthrough. He shared Jada's work with several of the guardians. He praised Lady Ashford for her expertise and Jada for her courage in owning up to the challenge of improving her skills. For the next few days Jada willingly wrote on the magic paper when given the opportunity. However, Master Poe and the other guardians responsible for her work did not incorporate the magic paper into her assignments.

By the end of the first week of the break through Jada began to realize that using the magic paper meant doing the work twice. When working with the Groundhog she began to cheat by writing with "tails" (g, p, q, y) above the line like every other letter. The confusion of the letters b and d returned. Her propensity to not close the lower case "a" and "g" and not place a vertical line on the letters "a, n and u" was more obvious. Although she was willing to make the corrections she could see that the reward for doing so was not worth the effort.

It occurred to the Groundhog that Jada might master writing more quickly if she practiced using the magic paper on the home front. Needless to say this was not a revelation as much as making a connection between her 20 minute nightly reading assignment and the required copying of a paragraph to the magic paper. Lady Ashford had indicated that the mere use of the paper would train Jada's eyes to correct the printing of her letters.

Over the course of the next two weeks Jada reported her daily progress to the Groundhog. Although she became more conscious of the need to complete the assignments her willingness to rewrite the completed work in order to earn the four stars did not materialize. The Groundhog continued to allow her to earn the two star ratings and began to look for external opportunities to engage her in her writing improvement project. He sensed that the year was coming to an end and that she had finally began to take some responsibility for her work. This indeed was a very positive turn of events because Jada had to unlearn the habit of being "lazy" and handing in whatever she scribbled on paper. Her feelings for the Groundhog made her willing to engage him with her work but her pattern of years of getting by while doing so little was hard to undue.

On her good days she purposefully did the work of the rewrites but on her lazy days she simply created obstacles to her own success. On the day that she finally earned a four star rating by correcting for spelling and doing the rewrite she shouted "yes" pumped her tiny fist and sprawled on the floor on her back. The Groundhog just smiled, marveling at her innocence and unbridled enthusiasm. This was the only moment in their entire time together that she demonstrated and feelings of excitement.

Critical and Unstable

The arrival of the warm weather seemed to bring new life to many of the associates and guardians throughout The Land Set Aside for Learning. The young associates could now go out and play and the guardians could take advantage of the same opportunity to go out and bask in the rays of the sun, seeking relief from the confines of the villages. Much of this rebirth was new to the Groundhog as he observed the spirit of the village take on a new aura. Even the usual suspects began to carry out their antics with greater enthusiasm.

Beneath this energy shift caused by the movement of the planet, the Groundhog came to see that the psychological state of the usual suspects in general and the Prophet and Friar Tuck in particular had remained critical. Out of some sense of eternal optimism or blind faith he had hoped that the brighter days would lead to lighter moments for the two. But, with each setting of the Sun he came to see that they had become joined during the coldest days of winter and now were tumbling into Spring with a sense of reckless abandonment.

In an apparent act of desperation, Master Poe had rearranged the village into a U-shape with Friar Tuck and the Prophet completely separated from the U and in opposite corners at the closed end. The Prophet was almost totally quarantined behind a 4 foot wall, kind of in his own ICU. Just over the wall the Groundhog perched each day. Friar Tuck's domicile was directly across so that he had to look through the Groundhog and over the wall to get a glimpse of approval from his most noble leader. Still the two of them were in continuous communication as the Friar wandered over to get a fix and check on the Prophet throughout the day.

Over the cold months the bottom had fallen out of Friar Tuck's small bowl of common sense. His alliance with the Prophet had caused him to lose his moral compass which guided him along the paths of the appropriate and inappropriate. He became disoriented and headed in the wrong direction. His smile of embarrassment and good nature had been buried under his new found joy of performing for the Prophet and Moses. Both the guardians and associates had grown to see and respond to him as almost incurable.

More so than any two characters encountered along the Groundhog's journey, the cold months in the Village of Poe had caused him to reexamine his understanding of the confluence of MIA fathers, peers and guardians. No two associates grew closer and exhibited less appreciation for Master Poe and the value of their time in the village. As the Prophet ceased to take refuge in the Zone of the Unreachable he found sustenance in the company of Friar Tuck. Their relationship with the Groundhog became one more stage for them to display the unstable condition of their personalities.

Whether in the Room for Eating, travelling along the by-ways of The Land Set Aside for Learning or in the Village of Poe, Friar Tuck sought the approval of the Prophet by conducting himself in a manner that earned him the reputation of being one of the least desirable male associates. Throughout the day the Prophet would mutter a stream of seemingly mindless disrespectful babble to gain the attention of the Groundhog and associates within earshot. Upon hearing the murmurings Tuck would seize the moment and wander over to join in the misadventure. Master Poe would question him about his objective in wandering and direct him back to his domicile. This worked momentarily but Friar needed a constant fix that only the Prophet could give him. Because the Prophet had skills his antisocial antics did not totally preclude his learning but for Friar Tuck, whose knowledge base was beneath the radar at the beginning of the year, the time spent under the spell put him off the charts in the improvement of his unstable condition.

As the Groundhog watched he wondered about what it would take to positively engage them in a recovery program. Their behaviors had put them at-risk of being hazardous to the health of all of the associates, not to mention the guardians. Their time in the Village of Poe had diminished the learning opportunities for all of the associates. In his heart he heard the immortal voice of Dr. King saying, "Sometimes I get discouraged, for indeed these are discouraging times." Like so many of the challenges he had seen there were no simple answers. To separate them into other villages would run the risk of spreading their condition and quite possibly facilitate their recruitment of new vulnerable associates. Isolating them within the walls of the Village of Poe was a sad temporary fix. Even though the weather had improved their condition remained critical and unstable.

A More Perfect Union

As the year grew closer to an end the Groundhog began to ponder what was next. Feeling less than successful about his efforts to impact the behaviors of the associates he decided to send out a call to the Towers of Learning in the Great Beyond. In his letter he wrote:

Day 150

Dear Colleagues,

I am desperately writing you at this time to solicit your interest, willingness and availability to participate in a journey that I have undertaken. You probably didn't realize it but it has been a year since my release. During the past year I have spent most of my days learning about the life of fourth year associates in the Village of Poe. Needless to say being around 8-11 year olds has been a lot different than the time I spent in the Women in Crisis Bureau. Most people who care to share seem to think I look younger as a result of my escape. Yes, it was always hard to tell the number of years that the Groundhog travelled the planet. One thing that is certain is that my service to the associates makes me a lot happier than the last two years of servitude under the Empress Katrina Shawshank. But enough about me, let's talk about you. Let me share what you can do for me.

I'd like to kick around some ideas about a project that would help you meet some of the mandates for the PK-4 guardian programs. What I have in mind is a summer project that could be designed as an education module running currently with a traditional summer school or as a stand alone enrichment module run like many of the summer enrichment camps. (By "enrichment" I mean empowering the have-nots, those with academic deficiencies, rather making the brightest brighter.)

As I mentioned, what's in it for you is that the program would address many of the PK-4 mandates contained in the electronic application. (I know I shouldn't bring that up.)

- New Guardian Support

- Collaboration and local school partnerships
- Pre-student teacher 75 hour practicum
- Faculty development/ applied research
- Family and Community Relations

It would be designed to address three primary objectives that I have discovered during my journey. 1) Remediate language arts skill deficiencies of young associates ages 8-11. 2) Develop instructional skills in the teaching of reading and writing of novice guardians with 1 to 3 years of guardianship. 3) Introduce pre-service guardians to small group and individualized instructional strategies, parent involvement and village management issues.

As presently conceived, the program would be a collaborative effort between a Tower of Learning and a place like The Land Set Aside for Learning. It would utilize one Tower faculty member, one novice guardian, four pre-service guardian candidates who will enter a full-time guardian training assignment the following year, and twenty associates divided between two villages. (The number of pre-service guardians and associates may vary but the ratio will not exceed 1 trainee to every five associates.)

The program curriculum will be developed by the Tower in collaboration with The Land Set Aside for Learning personnel in order to address issues related to curriculum and PSSA performance. It will be delivered during a five week summer session of 3 hours per day. The model would feature two periods of whole village instructional activities, let's say at the 9 and 11 o'clock hour. In between the two periods there would be small group and individualized activities. One day each week the pre-service candidate would meet during the middle block of time with one associate for 20 minutes and conduct an assessment activity. Assessments will be used to communicate ideas to parents about how to assist associates in addressing identified deficiencies.

The Land Set Aside for Learning would provide villages, one village for every ten associates, and supplies and equipment. The Tower would provide the faculty member and a three credit graduate scholarship to the novice guardian. Pre-service guardians would be expected to pay the costs negotiated by the Tower. Associates in the program would be expected to pay a nominal fee not to exceed $100. (Registration fees tend to encourage attendance and communicate a need for commitment to the parents.) If possible the proceeds from the registration fees would go to stipends for the pre-service candidates. The Land Set Aside for Learning would agree to accept two guardian trainees per semester the following school year.

That pretty much sums up the overall big picture of what I'd like for you to consider. I'm giving this letter to the the Land Set Aside for Learning administration as I am sending it to you. There is no implied commitment intended. I promise not to say anymore bad things about you if I don't hear from you. I'm simply trying to connect my past life and my new life and make a difference in the lives of some of the little associates that I have written you about. If logistics suggest that you can't bring your stuff this way feel free to take any of the ideas and develop partnerships where you are by molding any of the ideas that I have shared. I'd also welcome any thoughts that you could share about similar programs that you might be working on.

As I said in the beginning of this correspondence, I am growing desperate and in need of your assistance. I look forward to working with you. Too many of the associates are swimming against the current and going under so please step up and answer the call. There are many that still can be saved.

Be the change!

The Groundhog

Finding the Bottom

Late one afternoon the Prophet began calling out over the wall to the Groundhog. This call had become a part of his daily routine. He'd begin with comments on the Groundhog's attire or facial expression or posture. Inevitably his comments would escalate almost to a chant as the Groundhog intermittently responded or ignored the apparent mating call. However, on this day the Prophet was determined to gain the attention of the Groundhog and after a while the Groundhog gave in and inquired about the necessity of the chant.

Having secured the attention of the Groundhog the Prophet reverted back to his repetition of each statement. The Groundhog had come to understand that the repetition was the Prophet's way of conversing without having to process any ideas into thoughts. The conversation would go something like "Would you like to ask me something?" "No, would you like to ask me something?" "I thought you might be trying to get my attention." "I thought you might be trying to get my attention." "You're right I was trying to get your attention so that I could thank you for recognizing the shirt I was wearing." "I was not trying to get your attention to recognize the shirt you were wearing." This could go on indefinitely or at least until the Prophet became frustrated with the smile and politeness of the Groundhog.

But on this day the Prophet, not being satisfied with the usual repetitive discourse, reached deep into his bag of untouchables and pulled out the words that he was certain would shake the resolve of the Groundhog and earn his undivided attention. Very calmly he let the words "I'll beat the &%#* out of you!" fall from his lips. Having uttered them he immediately turned his head sideways, like a golfer trying to follow the trajectory of the ball in flight, and awaited the explosive impact on the Groundhog.

The Prophet's words were certainly surprising to say the least. If they had been delivered in the heat of an argument they may have been shocking but since they were shared almost for information purposes the Groundhog received them as if he were being told that his shirt collar was not buttoned correctly.

As he began speaking, the Prophet stared into his eyes looking for some sign of a battle that he was certain would come. Rather than going berserk and choking the daylights out of the Prophet, a response that would have brought great even though only temporary relief, the Groundhog whispered "You should be removed from the village for what you just said." The Prophet leaned forward straining his ears to hear more. He continued, saying that the repeated removals had not had the desired affect and appeared to only give him time away from The Land Set Aside for Learning. Then he suggested that the Prophet tell his father what he said because a father needs to know what his son is thinking. To that suggestion the Prophet began to slink away quietly mumbling that "Your father needs to know what you are thinking."

The following morning when the Prophet arrived at the village the Groundhog asked if he had shared his comment with his father. He said he had not. He asked him if he had told his mother. Again he said that he had not. The Groundhog then explained that he should share the comment with Friar Tuck, Moses and the Pretender so that they would know how he is thinking and get away from him. He went on to share that his comment suggested he was going in the wrong direction and taking them with him. The Prophet responded saying "You're going in the wrong direction." and walked away waving his hands in the air as if trying to keep a swarm of bees away.

The Groundhog stood up and watched, wondering if the Prophet had any idea of the level of disrespect his comment had reached. Did the Prophet know the power behind the thought of beating "&%#*" out of someone. Was this just something he had heard, maybe even directed at him, or did he harbor that level of anger towards the Groundhog? Unfortunately, the year was ending and to have travelled so far with the Prophet and end up at this juncture was troubling. There was little time for Plan B. The Groundhog just stood there quietly wondering about the swarm of bees around the Prophet's head.

Where were you?

Early one morning when the Groundhog awoke, rather than getting up, as was his usual custom, he decided to lay still and try to reconstruct a dream that was fading quickly. Normally the Groundhog's dreams were so vivid they would stay with him for days and allow more than ample opportunity for reflection. But the previous night's dream was different. He could only vaguely remember bits and pieces.

As he went about his daily routines he paused frequently to muse about the meaning of the dream. He remembered hearing the words "Where were you/?" Because he had been thinking about his failed efforts with the Prophet and Friar Tuck he wondered if the dream might have had something to do with Father Isle and the young associates' efforts to build a positive relationship with their fathers. Perhaps they had been crying out. He thought that maybe it had something to do with his distancing himself from them in order to make them show some sign of appreciation for his efforts and their education. Or, maybe it had to do with his trying to develop the enrichment program for associates that "wanted to learn" which in his heart he knew meant not the usual suspects.

He imagined himself and Master Poe in a transportation vehicle moving away from Father Isle and talking about what they had seen and commiserating over the walls that the young male associates had built to insulate themselves. He wondered if the two of them should have gained a better understanding of the associates which may have led to better relationships. Could it have been the voice of the Prophet lost in the Zone of the Unreachable and calling out and condemning everyone for not being there for him. Or, possibly Friar Tuck upset about the day his father was supposed to "drop by" the village and never showing up. Tuck may have finally gotten the opportunity to confront his father.

The more the Groundhog thought the more certain he became that he was constructing a story to go along with the words rather than gaining insight into the meaning. When the sun began to set he took time out from the various activities that he had been engaged in on this day when the gates of The Land Set Aside for Learning were closed.

As he sat gazing upon the flowers he had planted and the freshly cut grass, his thoughts turned to the mysteries of the seasons and how much he loved the end of the cold months. He began to drift off, lost in his thoughts, when the words came to him again. In an instant he knew the source of the words.

Somewhere in his inner being, his daily conversations with Master Poe, the antics of the Prophet and the evil spell-like manners of Friar Tuck had caused him to lose faith in the influence that they were having on the lives of the usual suspects. Although he continued to dress, and walk, and talk, and respond to the usual suspects in a manner that he hoped would provide them with an alternative model of a man, he questioned whether he was being effective because the year was coming to a close and he expected to see a change in their behavior. The change that he saw was far from what he had hoped for. Master Poe was anxiously anticipating bringing his first year in the village to a close and bidding them goodbye. They were demonstrating behaviors that suggested that negative attention was the best way to be the focus center for Master Poe and the Groundhog. Indeed they were all caught up in a battle that seemed to be coming to an end quicker than any had anticipated and the uncertainty of what was next was frightening.

With this insight came his understanding of the words that had been haunting him. He had been living with this over-inflated sense of the power of his presence in the lives of the usual suspects. He had not consciously processed the fact that it had taken Tuck and the Prophet ten years and hundreds of role models to condition them to wage the battles that they engaged in throughout The Land Set Aside for Learning. Instead of working like the farmer who toiled in the fields, continuing to water the unseen fruits of his labor, with no uncertainty about the pending harvest, somehow he operated under the misguided belief that he and Master Poe would undue all of the previous conditioning in less than a year. With a few weeks to go the combatants were assessing the outcome as if the struggle was over when in fact they had only been a part of a continuous series of skirmishes in each others lives.

In the rejuvenation of the plants the Groundhog could see a bigger plan about the ebb and flow of life. The words he had heard were not the voices of any of the usual suspects. They did not come from Father Isle. They were words of patience and encouragement from the One who created the seasons. They commanded him to be humble and find his place in the big scheme of things because even the coldest winter when all the trees are barren is followed by a bountiful spring. As he sat, he began to smile because he could hear the words more clearly and with greater certainty of the meaning, "Where were you when I created the foundations of the Earth?" He felt encouraged as his spirit rested with renewed determination for the coming days.

During the final weeks of the year he had many occasion to rejoice in the lessons he had learned during his journey. As he observed the associates he imagined what their futures would be like and prayed that somehow the usual suspects would find their way into lives that resembled the Three Musketeers rather than the Three Stooges. He saw Crown Jewel and Winnie giggling at the senior prom; Secret Squirrel and the Drummer going off to college together; the Rock in hospital scrubs; and Jada Pinkett becoming a writer of poetry. He wondered if they would remember the time that they shared in the Village of Poe and hoped that their memories would be pleasant.

Acknowledgments

In the weeks following my year in the Village of Poe I often thought about the many people who in so many ways made my journey possible. This final entry is a small reminder of how much I appreciated your support. I never would have made it without you.

At the top of my list is Paul Dronsfield who came into my life in 2002. Thank you for being with me for five of the six years of the reign of Marzilla Joykilla. Our daily walks, talks and laughter made it possible for me to endure Marzilla's emotional drain and accumulate enough time to retire with some semblance of financial security. The Mulberry Street Bridge is your monument.

Derek Coyle allowed me to come into his house everyday and do whatever was needed. Throughout the year he continued to try to reach a cast of characters that would have challenged and conquered the best of the guardians. His resolve to remain positive is a testament to his faith. I hope that someday you will look back and draw renewed strength from the Village.

The Land Set Aside for Learning is a place full of guardians who each day labor with enthusiasm to shape the lives of young associates. Few were the days during my journey that I stopped to share my reflections and concerns and could not find an open mind willing to point me in the right direction. I will always treasure the talks with Kathy Lee, Kathy Campbell, Carrie Martin, Barb Powell, Karen Love, Mike Selvenis and Ms. Ashley. They really don't pay you enough.

Each night that I sat down to write about the episodes that shaped my day, I was compelled to share my joy and frustrations with many of the faculty members from the Councils of the Knowing in the Great Beyond. Having you to talk with helped me to put into perspective the place that I left and the challenges of my new encounters. I hope that somehow my stories helped you in your work in preparing new teachers. Thanks for sharing and not hanging up or deleting my emails before responding. Kathy Ruthkosky, Carol Thon, Carol Pate, Kathy Kaminski, Greg Goodman, Kathy Nolan, Susan Munson, Ritchie Kelley, Michele Cheyne and Christina Shorall as it was in the Tower, so it was in the Village, your voices sustained me.

There are others, like Joseph Robinson, Jr., Cindy and Garvey Presley, Ira Blake, Pami Hagen, JoLynn Carney, Maureen Gillette and India Garnett whose daily lives are committed to service and who by word and example told me to keep going during those times when I had no idea where the road through the Land Set Aside for Learning was taking me. Thank you for helping me to see the usual suspects in the best light and to believe that my efforts have value.

As Paul so often said, in the end there is family, faith and friends. Vanessa, Aliyah and Naim had to hear more stories than I care to remember. My insomnia affected their lives and the spaces in my heart inhabited by the associates sometimes left little room for them. Thank you for seeing me through and allowing me to be the change that I hope for.

LaVergne, TN USA
19 November 2010

205635LV00001B/3/P